The Origins of Cannabis Prohibition in California

by Dale H. Gieringer, PhD

All rights reserved. No part of this book may be reproduced or used in any manner without the prior written permission of the copyright owner, except for the use of brief quotations in a book review. To request permissions, contact the publisher at angela@flowervalley.press. This book was originally published as "The Forgotten Origins of Cannabis Prohibition in California," in *Contemporary Drug Problems*, Vol 26 #2, Summer 1999 © Contemporary Drug Problems, Federal Legal Publications, New York 1999. Previous revisions and publications occurred in 2000, 2002, 2005, 2006, 2012, 2019, and 2022.

© 2024 Dale Gieringer, PhD
Berkeley, California
gieringer@comcast.net

Cover design by Estudio Creativo PI
Eighth edition 2024

ISBN: 979-8-9890163-6-5

FLOWER VALLEY
PRESS

Lompoc, California, United States of America
FlowerValley.Press

Acknowledgments

Thanks to Jim Baumohl, Richard Bonnie, Patricia Morgan, Jerry Mandel, Michael Aldrich, John Lupien, Isaac Campos, and Ellen Komp for their assistance in researching this material. Thanks to Andrew Garrett for the invaluable references provided in ReeferMadnessMuseum.org.

Table of Contents

Introduction	6
Early History of Cannabis in California	8
The First Stirrings of Cannabis Prohibition	44
The First Marijuana Busts	72
Prohibition a Bureaucratic Initiative	91
State & Local Marijuana Laws, Pre-1933	98
About the Author	101

Introduction

Although marijuana prohibition is commonly supposed to have begun with the Marihuana Tax Act of 1937, cannabis had already been outlawed in many states before World War I during the first Progressive Era wave of anti-narcotics legislation. California, a national leader in the war on narcotics, was among the first states to act in 1913. The tale of this long-forgotten law, predating the modern marijuana scene, casts light on the origins of 20th-century drug prohibition.

The 1913 law received no attention from the press or the public. Instead, it was promulgated as an obscure amendment to the state Poison Law by the California Board of Pharmacy, which was then pioneering one of the nation's earliest, most aggressive anti-narcotics campaigns.[1] Inspired by anti-Chinese sentiment, California was a nationally recognized leader in the War on Drugs. In 1875, San Francisco instituted the first known anti-narcotics

---

[1] The story of California's early war on narcotics and the State Board of Pharmacy has been largely neglected. Partial accounts may be found in: Jim Baumohl, "The 'Dope Fiend's Paradise' Revisited: Notes from Research in Progress on Drug Law Enforcement in San Francisco, 1875-1915," *The Driving and Drug Practices Surveyor* 24: 3-12, June 1992; Patricia Morgan, *The Political Uses of Moral Reform: California and Federal Drug Policy, 1910-1960* (PhD Dissertation, Univ. Cal. Santa Barbara, 1978); and Jerry Mandel, "Opening Shots in the War on Drugs," in Jefferson Fish, ed., *How to Legalize Drugs* (Jason Aronson Inc., Northvale, N.J., 1998), pp. 212-58.

law in the nation, an ordinance prohibiting opium dens, which was adopted by the state legislature in 1881. In 1891, the State Board of Pharmacy was created to oversee the practice of pharmacy, including the sale of poisonous drugs. In 1907, seven years before the US Congress restricted the sale of narcotics by enacting the Harrison Act, the Board quietly engineered an amendment to California's poison laws to prohibit the sale of opium, morphine, and cocaine except by a doctor's prescription. The Board followed up with an aggressive enforcement campaign, in which it pioneered many of the modern techniques of drug enforcement, employing undercover agents and informants posing as addicts, promoting anti-paraphernalia laws and the criminalization of users, and flaunting its powers to the public with a series of well-publicized raids on dope-peddling pharmacists and Chinese opium dens.

Early History of Cannabis in California

Throughout this era, "marijuana" was unknown in California. As a fiber crop, it was familiar to farmers at the time as hemp or *Cannabis sativa*. As a drug, it was known to pharmacists by its alternative botanical name, *Cannabis indica* (originally regarded as a different species). As an intoxicant, it was barely heard of, going by the name of hashish or Indian hemp, indulgence in which was an exotic vice of "Asiatic" foreigners and a handful of bohemians. "Marihuana," the Mexican name for the drug, was unknown in the state until the 20th century. Prior to this, the evidence for the use of hemp intoxicants in California is notably slim.[2]

---

[2] When this article was originally published in 1999, aside from a single story in the *San Francisco Call* (1895), the words "hashish," "cannabis" and "Indian hemp" did not appear in any California newspaper or periodical index prior to 1914. The situation has improved with the advent of the searchable online newspaper databases of the LA Times and California Digital Newspaper Collection, though evidence is still sparse. Presently, the first known reference to Mexican "mariguana" [not indexed] appears in the *Call* in 1897; the *LA Times* published four more articles about marihuana from 1898 to 1911; followed by a flock more when the Board began its anti-marihuana campaign in 1914. "Marihuana" does not appear in Northern California until the 1920s. Andrew Garrett's online library of early marijuana literature, www.reefermadnessmuseum.org, includes valuable references to early newspaper articles which are

Cannabis was initially introduced to California in the form of hemp by the Spanish, who cultivated it as a fiber crop at the Catholic missions.[3] Small-scale experiments with hemp cultivation continued sporadically into the 20th century in the

---

not indexed elsewhere, notably from the *LA Times.* The following indices were searched for this article: the San Francisco Newspapers Index (*Call* 1904–13; *Examiner* 1913–28; *Chronicle* 1913–28); *San Francisco Call* index 1894–1904; *Sacramento Bee* and *Union* index 1900–37; *Los Angeles Times* index 1912–27; *Marysville Appeal* index 1854–1967; *San Francisco Bulletin* index 1855–72; the Oakland Library Newspaper Index 1870s–1930s; the Stockton Library Newspaper Index 1870s–1920s; and the California Information File of the California State Library, which indexes several 19th-century periodicals and newspapers. The indices of the *San Diego Herald* and *Union*, and *Fresno Bee* turned out to be useless. The author also consulted the California newspaper drug index of the San Francisco *Chronicle* and *Examiner* for 1910–60 compiled by Pat Morgan for her PhD dissertation, op. cit., and the newspaper clipping collection of Jerry Mandel compiled from research and systematic samplings. Also searched were the *New York Times Index*, the El Paso Library newspaper index, the New Orleans Library newspaper index, and *Poole's Index to Periodical Literature,* 1802–1906. Finally, an invaluable reference was Ernest Abel's bibliography, *A Comprehensive Guide to the Cannabis Literature* (Greenwood Press, Westport, CT, 1979).

[3] Hemp culture was introduced to California at Mission San Jose in 1795 with the encouragement of Governor de Borica. It prospered thanks to Spanish subsidies, but collapsed with their end in 1810. Hubert Howe Bancroft, *History of California,* Vol. 1, p 717 and Vol. 2, pp. 178–81, (The History Co., San Francisco 1886); reprinted as Volumes XVIII and XIX of the *Works of Hubert Howe Bancroft* (Wallace Herberd, Santa Barbara, CA, 1963). Hemp was also cultivated by the Russians at Ft. Ross during the early nineteenth century: R.A. Thompson, *The Russian Settlement in California. Fort Ross. Founded 1812, Abandoned 1841. Why the Russians came and why they left.* (Oakland, Biobooks, 1951) pp. i–iv from Foreword (cited in personal communication by Michael Aldrich). A comprehensive report on hemp at the California missions may be found in U.C. Berkeley's Bancroft Library: J.N. Bowman, "Notes on Hemp Culture in Provincial California," (Berkeley, 1943).

Sacramento Valley and later Imperial County.⁴ There is no reason to suspect that either the Spanish or native peoples knew of its psychoactive or medical properties.⁵ American-grown *Cannabis sativa* was thought to have negligible psychoactivity, being thereby distinguished from medical-grade *Cannabis indica*, which was imported from India via England.

Cannabis indica became available in American pharmacies in the 1850s following its introduction to Western medicine by William O'Shaughnessy (1839).⁶ In its original

---

[4] Hemp cultivation experiments were proposed by Governor Bigler in 1850 and Governor Stanford in 1863, but foundered: Theodore H. Hittell, *History of California,* Vol. 4 (N.J. Stone & Co., San Francisco 1897), pp. 171, 369. Nevertheless, hemp continued to have boosters into the twentieth century ("California Should be Big Grower of Hemp," *San Francisco Call,* April 1, 1907, p. 8). As of 1909, some 300 acres of hemp were under cultivation in Butte County, according to the Statistical Report of the California State Board of Agriculture for 1916 (Appendix to Journals of the Assembly and Senate, 1917, p.66). The Imperial Valley became a center for experimentation with new hemp decortication equipment developed by George W. Schlichten in 1917: Don Wirtshafter, "The Schlichten Papers," in *Hemp Today,* ed. Ed Rosenthal (Quick American Archives, Oakland, CA 1994), pp. 47–62.

[5] Cannabis is absent from *Andrew Garriga's Compilation of Herbs and Remedies Used by the Indians and Spanish Californians together with some Remedies of his own Experience*, ed. Msgr. Francis J Weber (Archdiocese of Los Angeles, 1978). Father Garriga (1843–1915), who served at various missions in the Central Valley, compiled his collection around 1900–5 based on a manuscript by Fr. Doroteo Ambris, who died in 1883.

[6] O'Shaughnessy announced his discovery working in India in 1839. His discovery was reviewed in the *New York Journal of Medicine* 1 (3):390–398 in November 1843, but supplies of the drug were still scarce even in England at that time: "Remarks on Indian Hemp," (Unsigned) *New York Journal of Medicine* 2:273 (March 1844). In 1850, cannabis was listed as a "substance introduced into the materia medica" by the National Medical Convention in Washington D.C., in the *Pharmacopoeia of the United States of America*

pharmaceutical usage, it was regularly consumed orally, not smoked. The first famous American account of cannabis intoxication was published in 1854 by Bayard Taylor, author, world traveler and diplomat.[7] Though an easterner, Taylor had California connections, having ventured to the state in 1849 to write a popular Gold Rush travelogue, *El Dorado*. After returning home to New York, he departed for Egypt and Syria, where he encountered hashish. Having indulged his curiosity, he recounted his experiences in the manner of his French contemporaries of the *Club des Haschischins* in an article for *Putnam's* magazine and two books, *A Journey to Central Africa* and *The Land of the Saracens*.[8]

(Lippincott, Grambo & Co., Philadelphia, 1851) Around the same time, Frederick Hollick, a popular medical lecturer from Philadelphia, experimented with and successfully grew cannabis for himself, recommending it as an aphrodisiac in his *Marriage Guide* (NY, 1850): Michael Aldrich, "A Brief Legal History of Marihuana," (Do It Now Foundation, Phoenix, AZ c. 1970).

[7] Another early American account of cannabis intoxication is that of Kirtley Ryland, MD, "Experiments with Indian hemp - hashish," *Iowa Medical Journal*, Vol.2 #2 (Keokuk, Iowa, December 1854–January 1855), pp. 103–7.

[8] The Vision of Hasheesh," *Putnam's Magazine*, Vol. 3, April 1854, pp. 402–8; *A Journey to Central Africa* and (G.P. Putnam & Sons, NY, 1854) and *The Land of the Saracens* (G.P. Putnam & Sons, NY, 1855). On Taylor's life, see Ernest Abel, *Marihuana: The First Twelve Thousand Years* (Plenum Press, NY, 1980), pp. 172–4; and Arthur Quinn, *The Rivals* (Crown Publishers, NY, 1994), pp. 71–76, 104.

The Hasheesh Eater, by Fitz Ludlow (1857).

Fitz Ludlow (1836–1870)

14 Dale H. Gieringer, PhD

"Yesterday, Mark Twain and the Mouse-Trap man were seen walking up Clay street under the influence of the drug [hasheesh]."—*San Francisco Dramatic Chronicle*, September 18, 1865

Taylor's work was soon eclipsed by that of Fitz Hugh Ludlow, who created a sensation with what has been aptly described as the first psychedelic book, *The Hasheesh Eater* (1857).[9] Ludlow had become infatuated with the drug as a student at Union College in New York after trying a sample of Tilden's medicinal extract obtained from a pharmacist. Adopting the voice of a self-styled "Pythagorean" philosopher enthralled with the sublime harmonies of the universe, he expounded upon his hallucinogenic visions, alternating between ecstatic dreams of heaven and guilt-ridden nightmares of hell. After considerable trial and torment, he concluded with the successful resolve to "break away from the hasheesh thralldom." Having attained a degree of literary success that he would never again equal in his short career, Ludlow proceeded in 1863 to visit San Francisco, where he became an influential figure in literary circles, writing for the *Golden Era* and consorting with Mark Twain and Bret Harte. After a few weeks, he returned east, never to come back to California, dying of tuberculosis in 1870 at the age of 34.

While it is tempting to credit Ludlow with introducing hashish to California, there is no record

---

[9] Fitz Hugh Ludlow, *The Hasheesh Eater* (Harper & Bros., New York, 1857); reprinted in the Fitz Hugh Ludlow Memorial Library Edition, ed. Michael Horowitz (Level Press, San Francisco, 1975). Ludlow published an earlier, abbreviated account of his experiences in an article, "The Apocalypse of Hasheesh," *Putnam's Magazine*, Vol. 8, December 1856, pp. 625–40.

that he ever used the drug after finishing his book.[10] Still, the writings of the "Hasheesh Infant" were well known and admired in the state.[11] Sometime after his visit, the *San Francisco Dramatic Chronicle* reported, "It appears that a 'Hasheesh' mania has broken out among our Bohemians. Yesterday, Mark Twain and the 'Mouse-Trap' man were seen walking up Clay street under the influence of the drug, followed by a 'star,' who was evidently laboring under a misapprehension as to what was the matter with them."[12] Twain did not leave a first-hand account of his experience, though he alluded to hasheesh elsewhere in his writings. No further mention of San Francisco's 1860's "hasheesh mania" is known. However, there seems to have been some contemporary interest in Ludlow's work in the mining country.[13] In a brief note from Nevada

---

[10] Some biographers concluded that Ludlow relapsed and died from the hashish habit, but such a death is medically impossible. Ludlow wrote nothing more on hashish, but did write about the dangers of opium addiction: "What Shall They Do To Be Saved?" *Harper's Magazine*, Vol. 35 (August 1867) pp. 377–87. For biographies of Ludlow, see the Fitz Hugh Library Memorial Edition of *The Hasheesh Eater*, pp. 85–103 and Donald Dulchinos, *Pioneer of Inner Space: The Life of Fitz Hugh Ludlow, Hasheesh Eater* (Autonomedia, Brooklyn, 1998).

[11] Ludlow's book was sufficiently influential that copies of it were said to be "jealously guarded" by the University of California after two students took to hashish having read it. Franklin Walker, "The Hasheesh Infant Among the Argonauts," *Westways* 35: 18–20 (August 1935).

[12] *SF [Dramatic] Chronicle*, Sept 18, 1865. Like Twain, the "Mouse-Trap" man, aka Tremenheere Lanyon Johns, was a journalist for a rival newspaper. The "star" was likely a policeman. Ellen Komp, "Mark Twain's 'hasheesh' experience in SF," *San Francisco Chronicle*, October 2, 2011, p.E-9.

[13] Michael Aldrich reports obtaining an 1860 edition of Fitz Hugh Ludlow's book from a Placerville gold camp, "purchased by a miner

County, the *Chronicle* reported, "There is no amusement in Grass Valley, and several young men have in consequence taken to eating hasheesh."[14]

A few more sporadic stories about hasheesh may be found in the 19th-century California press, but they typically concern usage abroad, not in California.[15] One exception is an article on "Narcotics and Stimulants" in the *Daily Alta,* in which the reporter ventured to try hashish as well as smoking opium.[16] The experience turned out to be unpleasant. Like Ludlow, the author initially saw beautiful visions of fairyland but later descended into terrible horror, memory loss, and a headache. Despite this, the author claimed that the use of hashish "has made wonderful progress in the United States, there being some thirty thousand habitual smokers of the drug," an intriguing figure for which no source is cited. The author concludes that only alcohol and tobacco are "proper stimulants" and that

---

for his (married) sweetheart because, the inscription says, he couldn't find anything more interesting." M. Aldrich, "Hemp industry in California - Summary" (undated typed manuscript).

[14] *SF Chronicle,* Apr 27, 1867, p.3.

[15] For example, the French dramatist Jules Claretie reported on his harrowing experience with three Parisian friends in "Four Hours of Hasheesh" *San Francisco Call*, July 6, 1890.

[16] The article gave high usage estimates for other drugs too, claiming that out of 1,000 men, 950 use tobacco, 800 use "stimulants" of some kind; 200 use opium, morphine or hasheesh, etc "Narcotics and Stimulants," San Francisco *Daily Alta California* Vol. 24#8291, December 8, 1872, The *Tulare County Times* commented that the article's conclusions seemed "rather peculiar and questionable" (December 21, 1872, p.1).

the use of the others is "its own punishment." Such was the consensus of other contemporary observers.

One remarkable exception was a first-hand account published in the Virginia City *Territorial-Enterprise* under the title "Hashish: A Story for 1876."[17] The article is unsigned, but its style bears a strong resemblance to that of the paper's editor-in-chief, Rollin Mallory Daggett, co-founder of the *Golden Era*, a friend of Mark Twain, and later a Congressman and US minister to Hawaii. Unlike other contemporary accounts of hashish, such as Ludlow's, the author reports no negative feelings of terror or guilt but poetically describes rapturous visions he experienced under a dose of medically prescribed *Cannabis indica*. In a prophetic voice anticipating the counterculture of a century later, he rails against the materialistic excesses of the age: "Great corporations are gathering up your wealth... a love of wealth, of show, and a contempt for honest labor is growing up... men's ambitions have become both boundless and reckless." While Virginia City lay a few miles outside California in the mining country of Nevada, the article presages an appreciation of cannabis not otherwise evident in the literature of the state's Golden Age.

Cannabis preparations were readily available to Californians in pharmacies or via mail order.[18]

---

[17] Virginia City *Territorial-Enterprise*, January 9, 1876, p.1.

[18] According to Harry Hubbell Kane, a contemporary authority on drug use, "the English extract" of cannabis, imported from India, was regularly used both for intoxication and medical purposes (this is what Ludlow used): H H. Kane, *Drugs That Enslave: the Opium, Morphine, Chloral and Hashisch Habits* (Presley Blakiston, Philadelphia, 1881), pp. 207–8. Less commonly, non-pharmaceutical concoctions were used. Young Americans were

Hashish confections enjoyed a vogue after the publication of Ludlow's book and were advertised by Richards' Pharmacy in San Francisco in 1872.[19] In later years, such ads fell into disrepute, but pharmaceutical preparations were always available. The catalog of the San Francisco drug wholesale firm Redington & Co. listed "Fluid extracts of Indian hemp, (foreign) *Cannabis indica*," a "powerful narcotic," for $3 per pound c. 1880.[20] *Cannabis indica*

---

also said to chew on a "mixture of bruised hemp tops and the powder of betel, rolled up like a quid of tobacco," according to Mordecai Cooke in *The Seven Sisters of Sleep* (James Blackwood, London, 1860; reprinted by Quarterman Publications, Lincoln, MA, 1989) pp. 255–6.

[19] "MAGIC CONSERVES – Debilitated, Hypochondriac Sufferer, physically and mentally in need of an invigorator, pleasant and harmless, use this Hasheesh Confection" - $1 per box. *SF Chronicle,* September 19, 1872, p.2. The *Sacramento Union* ran a similar ad for "Magic Conserves" on October 17, 1872. An advertisement for hasheesh candy imported by the Gunjah Wallah Co. of New York, said to be from *Harper's Weekly*, October, 16, 1858, is reproduced in the Fitz Hugh Ludlow Memorial Library edition of *The Hasheesh Eater,* p. 201. Blatant ads of this sort came to be frowned upon by the pharmacy profession in later years. Warning that haschisch candy was used "much more generally than is commonly supposed," the editors of the *Boston Medical and Surgical Journal*, concluded, "If the manufacture of this candy cannot be prohibited or its sale restricted in this country by law, the public should at all events be made acquainted with its dangerous character." "Haschisch Candy," *BMSJ* 75:348-350 (November 22, 1866). According to the *New York World,* "At one time there was a prospect that hasheesh would come into general use, but the introduction into the market of a so-called "Hasheesh candy," which produced none of the desired symptoms of intoxication, brought the Oriental drug into complete disgrace": "Secret Use of Chloroform by Women," reprinted in the *Daily Alta California*, August 1, 1869.

[20] Redington & Co., "Revised Price List of Pharmaceutical Preparations," probably early 1880s: Bancroft Library, University of California, Berkeley.

continued to be advertised in pharmacy journals and catalogs until its prohibition in the 20th century.

The last quarter of the 19th century marked the high tide of popular drug use in America, an epoch later dubbed the "dope fiend's paradise." However, it was smoking opium, not cannabis, that originally emerged as the drug of interest to pleasure seekers in California. Introduced by the Chinese during the Gold Rush, the habit initially gave little offense. The situation deteriorated along with the economy in the 1870s when anti-Chinese sentiment rose, and the habit began to spread to whites, impelling San Francisco to enact the nation's first anti-narcotic statute, an ordinance outlawing public opium dens (1875). Other towns and states soon followed suit, including the California legislature (1881), as the nuisance spread across the country with the Chinese. Nonetheless, repeated legislative efforts failed to eradicate the habit but merely suppressed it from public view, leaving it to flourish in the back alleys of Chinatown and elsewhere for decades to come.

Meanwhile, on the East Coast, oriental-style hashish houses were said to be flourishing. An article in *Harper's Magazine* (1883), attributed to Harry Hubbell Kane, describes a hashish house in New York frequented by a large clientele, including males and females of "the better classes."[21] It goes on to say

---

[21] "A Hashish-House in New York," *Harper's Monthly*, Vol. 67: 944–9 (1883). Cf. the picture showing "Secret Dissipation of New York Belles: Interior of a Hasheesh Hell on Fifth Avenue," from the *Illustrated Police News*, December 2, 1876, reproduced in Solomon Snyder, "What We Have Forgotten About Pot," *New York Times Sunday Magazine*, December 13, 1970, p.26.

that parlors also existed in Boston, Philadelphia, Chicago, and especially New Orleans but fails to mention cities further west. Kane had previously written about the San Francisco opium scene in his book, *Opium Smoking in America and China*,[22] and might reasonably have been expected to know about hashish houses there. Yet despite the profusion of opium dens, bars, brothels, and gambling houses in San Francisco, there are no known contemporary accounts of hashish dens in California.[23]

Despite this lack of eyewitness testimony, an intriguing clue lies buried in the archives of the state law library in Sacramento among the musty volumes of bygone bills submitted to the California legislature. Numerous anti-narcotics bills were introduced during the 1880s and 1890s, most of which never reached a vote. Although they were mainly aimed at opium, three remarkably included hemp drugs as well. The first, introduced in 1880, entitled "an act to regulate the sale of opium and other narcotic poisons," would have made it unlawful to keep, sell, furnish, or give away any "preparations or mixtures made or prepared from opium, hemp, or other narcotic drugs" except on a

---

[22] H.H. Kane, *Opium Smoking in America and China* (G.P. Putnam's Sons, NY, 1882).

[23] In a well researched book without footnotes or bibliography, Larry Sloman provides no reference for his unsubstantiated claim that clandestine hashish clubs were operating in "every major American city from New York to San Francisco" by 1885: *Reefer Madness: The History of Marijuana in America* (Bobbs-Merrill Co., Indianapolis 1979), p.26.

written prescription at a licensed drug store.[24] Assemblyman A.M. Walker of Nevada County introduced it, yet further evidence of interest in hemp drugs in the mining country. Although the Walker bill was withdrawn from committee in favor of a competing anti-opium bill,[25] it may well rank as the first anti-cannabis bill in the United States.[26] An identical bill was reintroduced in 1885 by Assemblyman Peter Deveny of San Francisco,[27] and hemp drugs were included in another comprehensive anti-narcotics measure by Senator W.W. Bowers of San Diego in 1889, which also included cocaine.[28] Unfortunately, no record remains of any discussion of hemp drugs in

---

[24] AB 153, introduced January 17, 1880.

[25] *Sacramento Record Union,* March 3, 1880 p. 1.

[26] The first known anti-hemp bill actually passed in the US was an 1889 Missouri statute providing that every person who shall maintain any house, room or place for the purpose of smoking opium, hasheesh or any other deadly drug, shall be guilty of a misdemeanor (Section 3874, Revised Statutes, 1889): *British Medical Journal,* I June 5, 1897, p. 1092. In another, abortive attempt at anti-narcotics legislation, Indian hemp was included along with opium, cocaine, and chloral in two 1899 Tennessee bills to restrict the sale of narcotics to prescription only. Jeffrey Clayton Foster, "The Rocky Road To a Drug-Free Tennessee, A History of the Early Regulation of Cocaine and The Opiates, 1897–1913," *Journal of Social History,* Spring 1997, pp. 547–563.

[27] AB 223, introduced January 21, 1885. The bill was rejected by the Crimes and Penalties Committee on February 17. Another opium prohibition bill passed the legislature that year, but was vetoed by Governor Stoneman.

[28] SB 370, introduced January 25, 1889. The bill was reported favorably by the Committee on Public Morals on February 7 but never came to a vote. The bill is similar to an anti-narcotics ordinance enacted in San Francisco the same year, except that the latter mentioned only opium, morphine and cocaine, not hemp drugs.

connection with any of these bills. Indeed, although we have innumerable contemporary newspaper accounts of opium use in California, not a single story about hemp drugs from the 1880s is known. Likewise, while numerous towns passed anti-opium ordinances,[29] there are no known instances of local ordinances against hemp. Although the three stillborn bills in Sacramento clearly indicate some awareness and use of hashish in California, hemp drugs were never a serious public concern like opium smoking. They were most likely included for completeness rather than out of any pressing concern.

Further evidence of recreational hashish use in 19th-century California comes from a remarkable article in the *San Francisco Call*, dated June 24, 1895, which reported that Middle Eastern immigrants near Stockton were cultivating hashish:

> There are but few people in this State who know that "hashish," the opium of Arabs, is raised, prepared, smoked, and eaten in California the same as along the eastern shores of the Mediterranean and Red Seas. This astonishing information was made public yesterday by S.A. Nahon at the Board of Trade rooms...
>
> Mr. Nahon learned that the Arabs and Armenians or Turks are growing twenty acres

---

[29] In addition to San Francisco, opium dens were banned in Sacramento (1877), Stockton (1878), Oakland (1879), Marysville (1879), and ultimately by the state legislature (1881).

> of hemp near Stockton. They tell the farmers that it is for bird seed, but that is not all. They make and smoke kiff and send large quantities of hashish to this City for the use of the Turks and Arabs here, and large quantities are also sent to other parts of the United States where Arab and Turk hashish-eaters reside. The Stockton hemp farmers are making money fast by raising the drug and are keeping the secret away from their neighbors. Mr. Nahon proposes to enter the same field as soon as he can secure the land and make not only hashish for the Oriental consumers but the extract for the medicinal trade.

In a follow-up article, the *Call* continued (July 21, 1895):

> Among the new exhibits at the California State Board of Trade rooms on Market Street, is a product never before exhibited in California. It is Indian hemp, from which hashish is made. This sample came from a ten-acre patch growing near Livermore, Alameda County, and it was sent in by S. Nahon, who is familiar with the plant and its products.
> The Livermore field is being cultivated by several Arabs, who have for years been supplying their countrymen on this coast with the seductive drug. The business has been carried on quietly under the pretense that the hemp was used for canary bird seed.

> Mr. Nahon states that the hashish grown on this coast is much stronger or more rank in its opiate qualities than that grown in Arabia and India, due, he supposes, to the soil being less worked out than in the Orient. The Alameda-grown hashish is almost a deadly poison, it is so rank, and one smoking or eating the stuff is obliged to take it in homeopathic doses for fear of fatal results...
>
> Mr. Nahon states that there are several colonies of Arabs and Armenians in this State who raise hemp and send hashish in the natural and extract form to several parts of the United States, where their countrymen live.

There are slight discrepancies between the two articles. One puts the size of the field at 20 acres, the other at 10. One places it near Stockton, the other near Livermore; but the two cities are close, in the heart of the Central Valley's hemp-growing area. Most likely, the two fields were identical, although the article notes that several hashish farms existed in the state.

"Turks," "Arabs," and "Armenians" were terms interchangeably used to designate a group of Middle Eastern immigrants later known as the Syrians,[30] who had recently begun to immigrate to

---

[30] The category "Syrian" was introduced by US Immigration in 1899, prior to which these immigrants were referred to as Arabs, Turks, or sometimes Armenians or Greeks. Only 5,000 to 10,000 had reached the US as of 1895, almost entirely in the East. (Samir Khalef, "The Background and Causes of Lebanese/Syrian Immigration to the US Before World War I," in Eric Hooglund, ed.,

the US from the region around Lebanon, although their numbers in California were exceedingly small.[31] In addition to running tobacco factories and smoking parlors, the Syrians were reputed to be partial to hashish.[32] Whether the hashish farmers were truly Lebanese "Syrians" or came from some other, nearby part of the Ottoman Empire, they were certainly familiar with the indigenous hashish culture of the Middle East. A 20-acre plot could have produced a sizable yield: similar-sized pharmaceutical farms produced 10,000 to 30,000 pounds of medicinal cannabis.[33] Assuming an

---

Crossing the Waters: Arab-Speaking Immigrants to the United States Before 1940, Smithsonian Institution Press, Washington, DC, 1987, pp. 17–35).

[31] According to one reference, only 13 Syrians were living in California as of 1901! (Phillip M Kayal and J.M. Kayal, *The Syrian-Lebanese in America,* G.K. Hale & Co., Boston, 1975, pp. 81–3). A separate, more substantial Armenian immigration began to arrive in the state around 1896: James H. Tashjian, *The Armenians of the United States and Canada* (Armenian Youth Federation, Boston, 1947) pp. 18–21.

[32] The manager of the New York hashish house visited by Kane was said to be Greek, a name often used for Syrians. A so-called "Turkish Smoking Parlor," operated by "Turks or Armenians," i.e., Syrians, is pictured in the *New York Herald,* April 28, 1895, and reproduced in the underground hemp classic by Jack Herer, *The Emperor Wears No Clothes* (HEMP Publishing, Van Nuys, CA 1993), p. 65. Despite the implication that the patrons were smoking hashish, the article actually says they were smoking tobacco. It is unclear whether hashish might have been clandestinely offered at this establishment, or whether perhaps hashish and tobacco were smoked together. The Syrians' interest in cannabis is attested by Hamilton Wright, among others (see below). On Syrian involvement in the tobacco business, see Louise Seymour Houghton, "Syrians in the United States II: Business Activities," *The Survey,* August 5, 1911, pp. 654–5.

[33] WW Stockberger, "Commercial Drug Growing in the United States in 1918," *Journal of the American Pharmaceutical Association* 8:809 (1919).

average extraction ratio of 25 to 1, this would have yielded some 500 to 1000 pounds of hashish, or some 250,000 to 500,000 doses![34] Even if it supplied the entire US, it is hard to believe that the hash farm's clientele was entirely limited to the Arab-Syrian-Armenian community. Nonetheless, the Stockton hash farm disappeared from history without further trace.

In another curious, isolated report ten years later, the *Los Angeles Herald* reported a rise in hasheesh use among local spiritualists under the alarming headline, "Insanity caused by Hindoo drug—Result of Use of Hasheesh is Inevitable—Many Victims in Los Angeles."[35] The article is notable chiefly for documenting the fad for hashish among devotees of Oriental mysticism, which was then in vogue.[36] The article repeats familiar warnings about

---

[34] In 1984, Lebanese hash production was estimated at 700 metric tons for 20,000 hectares, or about 30 pounds per acre, which would work out to 600 pounds for the Stockton farm. Although extraction ratios nowadays can range upwards of several hundred to one for the finest, most potent hashish, it seems realistic to assume a lower average for commercial grades of the 19th century. Robert Connell Clark, *Hashish!* (Red Eye Press, Los Angeles, 1998) pp. 223, 233.

[35] *Los Angeles Herald*, May 14, 1905.

[36] Hashish had been popularized in spiritualist circles by Paschal Beverly Randolph and Madame Blavatsky during the late 19th century: Martin Lee, *Smoke Signals*, (Scribner, NY, 2012) p. 34. The link between spiritualism and hashish can be seen in another contemporary article from the *San Francisco Call*: "Psychic leaders have been given a severe jolt during the last fortnight, and a lot of society women are busy explaining at home how it all happened—those few "of them who let it be known at home that they frequent the perfumed chambers of Isis, to quaff drafts of hasheesh, that the veil of the unknown and unknowable may be lifted from the past and future." Sally Sharp, "The Occult Madness," *SF Call* Sept. 30, 1905.

the supposed link between hashish and insanity but fails to document a single actual user or victim of hashish insanity. No further accounts of LA's supposed epidemic of hashish insanity are known, most likely because it never occurred.

Literary testimony about hashish use in California is remarkably slim. Unlike their European counterparts, California's turn-of-the-century bohemian literati evinced little interest in drugs other than alcohol. One exception was Jack London, who confessed to "two memorable journeys" into "Hasheesh Land," "the land of enormous extensions of time and space," in *John Barleycorn*, his "alcoholic memoir" dedicated to the prohibition campaign (1913).[37] London was turned on to hasheesh by his poet friend George Sterling,[38] who led a bohemian

---

[37] Jack London, *John Barleycorn*, ed. John Sutherland (Oxford Press, NY, 1989) p. 185. The book was serialized in the *Saturday Evening Post,* where the passage about hashish first appeared on April 26, 1913. By this time, the Board of Pharmacy's anti-cannabis legislation had already been drafted.

[38] A boyhood friend, Frank Atherton, recalled London's account of a hashish trip with Sterling in 1903: "'To one who has never entered the land of hashish,' he said, 'an explanation would mean nothing. But to me, last night was like a thousand years. I was obsessed with indescribable sensations, alternative visions of excessive happiness and oppressive moods of extreme sorrow. I wandered for aeons through countless worlds, mingling with all types of humanity, from the most saintly persons down to the lowest type of abysmal brute.'" Russ Kingman, *Pictorial Life of Jack London* (Crown Publishers, NY 1979), p. 124. London tried hashish again on Guadalcanal during his famed yacht voyage on the *Snark* (1907). "He went clear out of his head and acted so wild that Charmian [his wife] was frightened. That was the end of the hashish experiment. Nobody else would touch it." *Ibid.* p. 202. See D. Gieringer, "Jack London, California Cannabis Pioneer," *Oaksterdam News,* March 2005, posted at http://www.canorml.org/history/London-CannabisPioneer.pdf

artist colony in Carmel. Sterling was familiar with other drugs and drink, but left no account of his hasheesh experiences.[39] Altogether, California's cannabis literature amounts to just a few brief references, hardly enough to impart a meaningful impression.[40]

The best scientific sources of information on cannabis in California are West Coast pharmacies and medical journals such as the *Pacific Pharmacist* and *Pacific Drug Review*.[41] Most of the references are

---

[39] A solitary passing reference to cannabis may be found in Sterling's Carmel diary: "January 16 [1906]. Stormy. Gene & Toddy took hashisch." Further details of their experience are lost to history. Franklin Walker, *The Seacoast of Bohemia* (Peregrine Smith, Inc., Santa Barbara, CA 1973), p. 28. On Sterling's drug use and alcoholism, see Joseph Noel, *Footloose in Arcadia* (Carrick & Evans, NY 1940), pp. 162–5.

[40] One other California bohemian, Charles Warren Stoddard, coyly mentioned a possible encounter with hasheesh on a visit to Egypt. "The April heat was increasing in Grand Cairo. Under its enervating influence, I subsided into a hasheesh frame of mind, and passed my time between the bath and the nargileh, the victim of brief and fitful moods." C.W. Stoddard, *Mashallah! A Flight Into Egypt* (Appleton, NY 1881), p. 217; also pp. 141–2, 184–5.

[41] Unfortunately, many of the pharmacy trade publications from the turn of the century are lost. Following are the survivors to be found in the University of California's MELVYL library system, which were surveyed for this article: *The Pacific Pharmacist* (San Francisco, 1907–1918); *Pacific Drug Review*. (Portland & San Francisco 1905–1915); *San Francisco and Pacific Druggist* (Coffin & Redington Co., SF 1910–4); *The Drug Clerk's Review* (San Francisco, incomplete, misc. issues 1911–4, 1918); *Pacific Druggist* (SF, incomplete, misc. issues 1892, 1894); and, from the Smithsonian Annex Library, *California Druggist* (LA, 1896–1901). The following medical journals were surveyed: *Pacific Medical & Surgical Journal* (San Francisco, 1858–1915); *Occidental Medical Times* (Sacramento, 1887–1904), *Pacific Record of Medicine and Surgery* (San Francisco, 1886–

minor notes or reprints of articles concerning medical use. Unlike the East, where numerous physicians investigated and wrote about cannabis, California was not a center of medical cannabis research.[42] Medical interest in cannabis was declining by the turn of the century, largely due to uncertainty over its potency, activity, and effects.[43] By 1910–14, it was no longer advertised in the Coffin & Redington house organ, *San Francisco and Pacific Druggist*. A survey of medicinal plants in California by Professor Albert Schneider of the California College of Pharmacy noted that, while cannabis hemp could be found growing wild in Butte County, the "exact medicinal value of the California-grown plants requires further careful study."[44] However, Professor Schneider was not interested enough to mention *Cannabis indica* in a list of 26 varieties of

---

1899), *Califonia State Journal of Medicine* (San Francisco, 1904–1913), *California Medical Journal* (Oakland, 1880–1888).

[42] Californians are absent from the compilation of biographies of prominent 19th-century cannabis researchers in Tod Mikuriya, *Marihuana: Medical Papers 1839–1972* (Medicomp Press, Oakland, CA, 1973), pp. 446–9. The dozen articles about cannabis published in 19th-century California medical journals are reprints or reports from Europe, with the exception of an account, "Poisoning by Strychnia, Successfully Treated by Cannabis," by Stacy Hemenway, MD of Eugene City, Oregon, in the *Pacific Medical and Surgical Review* 10: 113 (August 1867).

[43] "*Cannabis Indica* has fallen greatly into disuse in this country, and it matters little to us whether the drug is produced in Asia, Africa, or America. Quite possibly this lack of interest has been brought about by our failure to ensure that our preparations are always active." *Chem. and Druggist*, cited in *The Pacific Pharmacist* 6:177 (November 1912).

[44] *The Pacific Pharmacist* 1:467 (January 1908).

drug plants being considered for cultivation in California.[45]

---

[45] "Drug Plant Culture in California," *Pacific Pharmacist*. 3: 184–94 (October 1909). Although apparently uninterested in medical cannabis, Professor Schneider later created a stir at the University of California by experimenting upon himself with hashish, "explod[ing] the theory that the drug has a fatal effect upon any but Orientals." "Professor Takes Hashish; Goes on Scientific Toot: Walks About Town Acting Perfectly Natural, But Is 'Extremely Happy,'" *Daily Californian,* July 8, 1921, p. 1.

Hindoo Sea Serpent–Cartoon and article from the SF Examiner, August 9, 1910

It is unlikely that cannabis was ever grown for medicine in California until modern times. Up to World War I, pharmaceutical supplies of *Cannabis indica* were regularly imported from India (and occasionally Madagascar) in accordance with the US Pharmacopoeia, which specified that it come from flowering tops of the Indian variety.[46] American varieties from Kentucky and the Southeast were also occasionally available under the name "*Cannabis americana*," but were thought to be of inferior quality.[47] The principal active agent of cannabis, tetrahydrocannabinol, being still undiscovered, there was great uncertainty about its medical activity, which had to be tested in animals. Finally, in 1913, the US Department of Agriculture Bureau of Plant Industry announced it had succeeded in growing domestic cannabis of equal quality to the Indian.[48] When foreign supplies were interrupted by World War I, the United States became self-sufficient in cannabis. By 1918, some 60,000 pounds were being produced annually, all from pharmaceutical farms east of the Mississippi.[49] Not until the 1990s

---

[46] An early reference to *Cannabis americana* is John B. Biddle, *Materia Medica for the Use of Students*, 6th Edition, Philadelphia 1874.

[47] R. H. True and G.F. Klugh, "American-Grown Cannabis Indica," *Proceedings of the American Pharmaceutical Association* 57:843–7 (1909); E.M. Houghton and H.C. Hamilton, "A Pharmacological Study of *Cannabis Americana* (*Cannabis sativa*)," ibid., 55: 445–8 (1907).

[48] *Pacific Drug Review* 25(8):40 (August 1913).

[49] W.W. Stockberger, "Commercial Drug Growing in the US in 1918," *Journal of the American Pharmaceutical Association*. 8:809 (1919).

and the rise of the medical marijuana movement in San Francisco would California become a major center for medicinal cannabis production.

On rare occasions, articles in pharmacy and medical journals discussed cannabis as an intoxicant, typically in foreign contexts. In the waxing prohibitionist climate of the Progressive Era, interest in hashish was definitely *démodé*. Dr. Victor Robinson created a minor stir with his "Essay on Hasheesh," published in the *Medical Review of Reviews* (1912), in which he approached the subject with the same open-minded curiosity as O'Shaughnessy and Bayard Taylor.[50] In a brief review, the *Pacific Pharmacist* commented that hasheesh "seemed to appeal to the oriental mind," not exactly a ringing endorsement in a state rife with anti-Asian prejudice.[51]

In the meantime, a new drug menace had begun to infiltrate from Mexico: "marihuana." The term refers specifically to cannabis leaf smoked in cigarettes, at that time a novel form of delivering the drug. Unlike pipes and cigars, cigarettes were singled out by temperance advocates as a morally suspect form of smoking.[52]

---

[50] V. Robinson, "An Essay on Hasheesh," *Medical Review of Reviews* 18:159–69 (1912).

[51] Review of "An Essay on Hasheesh," *Pacific Pharmacist* 6:127 (Sept. 1912).

[52] Several states, but not California, passed cigarette prohibition laws in the years before World War I. See Cassandra Tate, *Cigarette Wars: The Triumph of 'The Little White Slaver,'* Oxford U. Press (1999).

The origins of marihuana use in Mexico are obscure.[53] Perhaps the first American newspaper reference to Mexican "mariguana" appears in a Southwest travelogue published by the *San Francisco Call* (1897):[54]

> In Southern Arizona, the jail and prison officials have their hands full in trying to prevent the smuggling into their institution of the seductive mariguana. This is a kind of loco weed more powerful than opium. It is a dangerous thing for the uninitiated to handle, but those who know its users say it produces more raising dreams than opium. The Mexicans mix it with tobacco and smoke it with cigarettes, inhaling the smoke. When used in this way, it produces a hilarious spirit in the smoker that cannot be equaled by any other form of dissipation...

---

[53] According to Isaac Campos, the first known Mexican report of marihuana smoking appeared in *El Republicano* (Mexico City) April 5, 1846. Campos, op. cit., p. 73, fn 29.

[54] "It Brings Ravishing Dreams of Bliss," *San Francisco Call*, October 24, 1897, p. 17. The article was reprinted by various other newspapers. ReeferMadnessMuseum.org lists the following other early newspaper references to marihuana: *New York Times*, "Doctors of Ancient Mexico," January 6, 1901, p. 18; the *Washington Post*, "Terrors of Marihuana" (referring to it as the hasheesh of Venezuela), March 21, 1905, p. 18; and the *Los Angeles Times*, "Delirium or Death," (reprinted from the *Mexican Herald)*, March 12, 1905, p. V 20; and *Los Angeles Times*, "Hasheesh" (likening Mexican "mariguana" to the hasheesh of India), November 17, 1908, p. 13.

Shortly afterward, "mariguana" was said to be growing in Southern Arizona, prompting the *San Diego Tribune* to remark, "San Diego ranchers now raise excellent tobacco, but it is to be hoped that they will not experiment in the culture of mariguana."[55]

From its earliest origins in Mexico, marihuana had an alarming reputation for provoking madness and violence, as documented by Isaac Campos in his history of marijuana in Mexico.[56] This popular view is reflected in the following story from the *Pacific Drug Review* (1906):[57]

---

[55] *San Diego Tribune* report reprinted in an untitled article in *Los Angeles Times*, January 8, 1898, p. 6.

[56] Isaac Campos, *Home Grown: Marijuana and the Origins of Mexico's War on Drugs* (University of N. Carolina Press, 2012).

[57] The article was printed in the *Pacific Drug Review* 18(4):6 (April 1906) as a reprint from *The Spatula*. The same article was attributed to the Alumni Report of the Philadelphia College of Pharmacy, November 1905, in a letter from the Manufacturing and Biological Chemists of Philadelphia to G. E. Hesner, Superintendent of the Corozal Hospital, Panama City, reprinted in the Panama Canal Zone report, "Report of Committee Appointed by the Governor April 1, 1925 for the Purpose of Investigating the Use of Marihuana and Making Recommendations Regarding Same and Related Papers," 1925 (photocopy from U. of Virginia Law Library). A humorous poem entitled "Marihuma" [sic]was published in the British magazine *Punch*, April 5, 1905. It begins: "Flower of the West with the soft, sweet, name, / Marihuma/Follow, oh follow thy new-won fame, /Marihuma." Another early account, "Terrors of Marihuana," in the *Washington Post*, March 21, 1905 p. 6, links marihuana to "super-human, soul-bursting" feats of valor by Latin American revolutionaries. Earlier still, the *New York Times* mentions Mexican folk healers who "baffle the government by bringing in the Marihuana, which sends its victims running amuck": "Doctors of Ancient Mexico," *New York Times*, January 6, 1901 p. 18; datelined "City of Mexico, December 27, 1900." A dubious reference to a spell-casting herb called "mariguan" in *Scribner's* from May 1894, is said to be the earliest English-language reference to marijuana, according to the *Dictionary of American English* (Ed. Craigie & Hulbert, 1942).

Mariahuana [sic] is one of the most dangerous drugs found in Mexico. The weed grows wild in many localities of the southern part of that country. Its wonderful powers as a[n] intoxicant have long been known to the natives and many are the wild orgies it has produced. So dangerous is mariahuana, writes a correspondent to the *Sun,* that in the City of Mexico and other Mexican cities, the Government keeps special inspectors employed to see that the weed is not sold in the markets.

A few years ago, it was found that many prisoners in the Belem prison in the City of Mexico were losing their minds. An investigation was started and the discovery was made that they were all addicted to the use of mariahuana, which was smuggled in to them by the guards, who had been bribed for that purpose. Since then strict orders prohibiting the use of mariahuana by prisoners have been enforced.

The poisonous weed always finds favor among the soldiers, who mix it with tobacco and smoke it. The sale of the weed to the soldiers is strictly prohibited, and severe punishment is provided for anyone guilty of the offense.

The habitual user of mariahuana finally loses his mind and becomes a raving maniac. There are scores and scores of such

> instances in Mexico. It is said that those who smoke mariahuana frequently die suddenly.
>
> The smoking of mariahuana is a seductive habit. It grows upon a person more quickly and securely than the use of opium or cocaine...

One of the earliest reports about marijuana on US soil concerned its cultivation for medical purposes in Texas, as reported in the *Pacific Drug Review* (1909):[58]

> James Love, who conducts an agricultural experimental station near Cuero, Texas, has been granted special permission by the State Agricultural Department to introduce the deadly Marihuana plant from Mexico into Texas. He has therefore obtained several pounds of seed and believes that the plant can be put to good commercial use as a drug, to be used in the cure of asthma, tuberculosis, etc. The marihuana weed is known as the most harmful of narcotic influences, however, and its leaves, when smoked in the form of cigarettes, produce a species of insanity which frequently ends in a horrible death. It is said that Empress Carlotta, the wife of Emperor Maximilian, had her mind dethroned by drinking coffee in which marihuana leaves had been placed. She left Mexico an incurable lunatic at the time of the overthrow of the

---

[58] "Marihuana to be Grown in Texas," *Pacific Drug Review* 21(5):68 (May 1909).

French in that country, and has never regained her faculties.[59] When used in a legitimate way it is possible to force this deadly thing to prolong life rather than to sap it, and Mr. Love is working to this end.

Remarkably, neither of the preceding articles explained that the deadly marihuana was precisely identical to *Cannabis indica*. This fact might well have surprised readers, given cannabis' reputation for pharmaceutical safety. Although overdoses of cannabis were known to induce temporary quasi-psychoses and non-fatal poisonings, cannabis was never regarded as a deadly drug. "Who ever heard of anybody being killed with cannabis indicas...?" scoffed the *Pacific Pharmacist,* criticizing a proposed anti-narcotics bill that would have required a death's head to be marked on a sweeping list of purported poisons.[60] However, hashish was reputed by medical journals to be a common cause of insanity in the Middle East, where it was sometimes linked to

---

[59] Carlotta's madness did not appear until after her return to Europe, and thus cannot be credibly attributed to marijuana (this myth may have its origins in the fact that she fantasized about being poisoned). Egon Corti, *Maximilian and Charlotte of Mexico*, Vol. 2, Chap X (Knopf: New York and London, 1928). The Carlotta legend appears in a different form in another article, "Plants Cause Madness: Startling Effect of Mexico's Substitute for Tobacco," printed in the *Washington Post,* March 9, 1913 p. MT-3. There it is stated that she was poisoned by a tea made from seeds of "totrache," a relative of "loco" weed.

[60] "Do We Want the Mann Bill?," *Pacific Pharmacist* 2:305 (December 1908).

homicide and death.[61]

Still, nothing could compare with the frightful, though scientifically unjustified, reputation of Mexican "marihuana" for producing madness, violence, and death. The explanation lies in the fact that marijuana was widely considered to be a lower-class drug in Mexico. By the turn of the century, it had come to be associated chiefly with delinquents and freelance soldiers, which naturally enhanced its reputation for promoting violence.[62] According to a report from the *Mexican Herald* published in the *LA Times*:[63]

> Marihuana is a weed used only by people of the lower class and sometimes by soldiers, but those who make larger use of it are prisoners sentenced to long terms...
>
> The drug leaves of marihuana, alone or mixed with tobacco, make the smoker wilder than a wild beast... Everything, the smokers say, takes the shape of a monster, and men look

---

[61] Dr. A.W. Hoisholt, of the State Asylum for the Insane in Stockton, noted a British report on "Insanity from the Abuse of Indian Hemp," in *Occidental Medical Times* 8:197 (1894). Hasheesh was said to be the "most frequent cause of lunacy in Egypt": F.W. Sandwith, "Insanity from the Abuse of Indian Hemp," *Occidental Medical Times* 3:142 (1889).

[62] Ricardo Pérez Montfort, "Fragmentos de historia de las 'drogas' en México 1870–1920," in Montfort, ed. *Hábitos, normas y escándalo* (CIESAS-Plaza y Valdés, México, 1997), pp. 187 ff.

[63] "Delirium or Death: Terrible Effects Produced by Certain Plants and Weeds Grown in Mexico," *Los Angeles Times*, Mar. 12, 1905, p. V20.

like devils. They begin to fight, and of course, everything smashed is a "monster" killed...

People who smoke marihuana finally lose their mind and never recover it, but their brains dry up and they die, most of the time suddenly.

In an early "Reefer Madness" story, the *LA Times* reported that an unknown Mexican, allegedly crazed by "mariguana" approached the border at Nogales, Arizona, brandishing a revolver, and was shot dead by Mexican police.[64]

Fittingly, perhaps the earliest report of "mariguana" cultivation on California soil was in San Quentin prison, where inmates were said to grow Indian hemp from canary seed, much to the disgruntlement of prison officials, who banished the inmates' canaries and strove to "dig out every weed on the grounds."[65]

Marihuana was used by troops in the Mexican Revolution of 1910-20, whence it is said to have infected American troops along the border.[66] Popular legend would have it that it was especially popular with the notorious raiders of Pancho Villa,

---

[64] "Hasheesh," *LA Times*, 17 November 1908 p.3.

[65] "Canary Bird's Food Is Convict's Dope," *Minneapolis Tribune*, 17 July 1904. (California news source unknown).

[66] "One of the things to be avoided by American soldiers in Mexico is the seductive marihuana weed, which grows around Vera Cruz": "Weeds Cause Insanity," *Los Angeles Times*, July 1, 1914, p.18. Bonnie and Whitebread, *The Marihuana Conviction*, pp. 32–8; Robert P Walton, *Marihuana, America's New Drug Problem* (J.B. Lippincott, Philadelphia, 1938), p. 25.

whose anthem, *La Cucaracha,* contained a celebrated verse about marihuana.[67] Villa himself did not drink, smoke, or use drugs and was praised for closing down liquor stores, but his views on marihuana have not been recorded.[68] No doubt, marihuana was used by Mexican soldiers of all stripes, although contemporary journalistic evidence is scanty.[69]

---

[67] "La cucaracha/ ya no puede caminar/ porque no tiene/ marihuana que fumar." This verse about the "cockroach" who can't go on without marihuana has often been interpreted as a celebration of marihuana. More likely, it was a derisive satire against the reviled Mexican dictator Victoriano Huerta, the "cockroach," who was said to abuse drugs and alcohol: Isaac Campos, *op.cit.,* pp. 161–3. For the Villista marijuana legend, see Walton, op. cit. p. 25; Ernest Abel, op. cit., p. 201; Daniel Skye, "Riding High With Pancho Villa," *High Times*, April 1998, pp. 52ff.

[68] Friedrich Katz, *The Life and Times of Pancho Villa* (Stanford University Press, CA, 1998), pp.76, 477; Ernest Otto Schuster, *Pancho Villa's Shadow* (Exposition Press, NY, 1947), introduction; Louis Stevens, *Here Comes Pancho Villa* (Fred Stokes Co. NY, 1930), pp. 109, 111–112. Evidence of Villa's views on marihuana is absent from documents of the revolutionary period, according to Professor Friedrich Katz (personal communication). Lurid tales of marijuana-crazed Villistas were published later, after the "Reefer Madness" era had commenced, e.g., Haldeen Braddy, *Cock of the Walk: Qui-Qui-Ri-Quí! The Legend of Pancho Villa* (Kennikut Press, Port Washington, NY 1970; orig. ed 1955) pp. 113, 119–20, 148–9, and Pablo Osvaldo Wolff, *Marihuana in Latin America* (Linacre Press, Wash. D.C. 1949), pp. 22–3.

[69] Marihuana use was reported among the rowdy and drunken troops of Villa's crony General Che-Che Campos, whereas order was said to reign among Villa's own troops, where liquor was banned: "Rapine in Wake of Rebel Army," *Indianapolis Star*, April 28th, 1914. p. 4. According to the *Los Angeles Times*, "A large proportion of Mexican officers as well as men are dope fiends. They smoke marihuana" ("Government of Carranza on Last Legs," September 1, 1919, p. 12). President Huerta banned marihuana smoking in the army: "Edict Against Seductive Weed," *Los Angeles Times,* November 28, 1920, p.IV 1. For more on marihuana use in Mexico, see Benjamin T. Smith, *The Dope: The Real History of the Mexican Drug Trade,* (W.W. Norton, 2021).

Not until the anti-dope campaigns of the 1920s and 30s did marihuana become familiar to the general public. By this time, pharmaceutical cannabis had fallen into disuse, and the myth of Reefer Madness gained ascendancy thanks to such able propagandists as William Randolph Hearst, Colonel Richmond Hobson, and Harry Anslinger. Nonetheless, it was never fully accepted by the medical profession, which would repeatedly voice skepticism over the vaunted dangers of marijuana in the Panama Canal Zone report (1925), the Marihuana Tax Act hearings (1937), the LaGuardia report (1945), and elsewhere.[70]

As of 1910, however, "marihuana" was still so obscure that it played no role in the original debate over federal drug legislation. Instead, the initial debate was focused on its more familiar manifestations as *Cannabis indica*, alias Indian hemp, or hashish.

---

[70] The Canal Zone Report was not published, but may be found in the University of Virginia Law Library; the Marihuana Tax Act hearings may be found in *Taxation of Marihuana*, House Committee on Ways and Means, 75th Congress, 1st Session. (April 27–30 and May 4, 1937); the LaGuardia Report, by the Mayor's Committee on Marihuana, was published as *The Marihuana Problem in the City of New York* (Jacques Cattell Press, Lancaster, PA, 1944).

The First Stirrings of Cannabis Prohibition

The first laws against cannabis were byproducts of the broader national anti-narcotics movement. Fueled by Progressive Era faith in government-supervised moral reform and growing prohibitionist sentiment, the movement reached critical mass in 1906, when the US, British, and Chinese governments came to a consensus on the need to control opium traffic. This would culminate in international conferences in Shanghai (1909) and the Hague (1912), where the groundwork for international drug prohibition would be laid.

The year 1906 also saw the passage of the first federal drug legislation, the Pure Food and Drugs Act. Essentially a truth-in-labeling law, the Pure Food and Drugs Act was the first federal law to mention *Cannabis indica*, including it with alcohol, opiates, cocaine, and chloral hydrate on a list of intoxicating ingredients whose presence was required to be noted on the label.

In response to the federal lead, California's new Governor, James Gillett, proposed in his inaugural address that the state adopt drug legislation of its own. The legislature duly responded by enacting not only a pure food and drugs law but also a little-publicized amendment to the state poison law, drafted by the Board of Pharmacy, prohibiting the sale of opium, morphine, and cocaine except by a physician's prescription (1907), laying the basis for California's subsequent War on Drugs. Immediately thereafter, the Board began dispatching agents from city to city, cajoling dope from unwitting pharmacists and arresting them. As the war heated up, the narcotic laws were expanded to prohibit possession as well as sales (1909), forbid refills and prescriptions to addicts (1909), and outlaw opium paraphernalia (1911). In a dramatic display of its powers, the Board made the front page of the *San Francisco Examiner* with a massive public bonfire of opium paraphernalia in the middle of Chinatown.[71]

Meanwhile, federal anti-narcotics efforts had been put in the hands of the brash and energetic Hamilton Wright, whom President Roosevelt appointed to direct narcotic affairs from the State Department.[72] In preparation for his task, Wright took it upon himself to conduct a nationwide survey of police, universities, pharmacies, boards of health, and other institutions concerning narcotics use.[73] Among other things, Wright asked about cannabis. One of the surviving responses preserved in the

---

[71] "Sad Chinatown Sees $20,000 Opium Bonfire: Mourners Gaze on Hissing Funeral Pyre," *San Francisco Examiner*, May 10, 1912, p.1.

[72] David F. Musto, *The American Disease: Origins of Narcotic Control* (Yale Univ. Press, New Haven, 1973), pp. 31–3.

[73] Peter D. Lowes, *The Origins of International Narcotics Control* (Librairie Droze, Geneva 1966), p. 100.

National Archives is from the police department of San Francisco, which reported: "There has been only one case of the use of Indian hemp or hasheesh treated in the Emergency Hospitals in six years, and that was accidental"[74] (presumably an overdose).

Although Wright found no public interest in cannabis in his survey, he nonetheless saw good reasons for its inclusion in the first draft of his proposed anti-narcotics bill, which would evolve into the Harrison Act.

> In passing a Federal law that will prevent undesirable drugs, it will be necessary to look well into the future. I would not be at all surprised if, when we get rid of the opium danger, the chloral peril and the other now known drug evils, we shall encounter new ones. The habitués will feel that they must adopt something to take the place of the 'dope' they have lost through legal enactment. Hasheesh, of which we know very little in this country, will doubtless be adopted by many of the unfortunates if they can get it.[75]

With this in mind, Wright pressed to have cannabis included in the initial draft of national narcotics legislation along with cocaine and opiates.

---

[74] Letter from Sgt. Arthur Layne to Capt. Thomas S. Duke, June 26, 1909, sent by the SF Chief of Police to Hamilton Wright in response to a letter of inquiry from the US Opium Commission, in the National Archives, Record Group 43, Records of US Delegation to the International Opium Commission and Conferences of 1909–13 and Records of Hamilton Wright.

[75] "Nations Uniting to Stamp Out the Use of Opium and Many Other Drugs," *New York Times Magazine*, July 25, 1909.

This proposal was ill-received by the pharmaceutical manufacturers, who objected to the inclusion of a seemingly harmless ingredient of proprietary medicines.[76] Cannabis was ultimately dropped from the Harrison Act in May 1913; federal legislation would wait until the 1937 Marijuana Tax Act.[77]

---

[76] David Musto, "The Marihuana Tax Act of 1937," *Archives of General Psychiatry* 26: 101-8 (February 1972).

[77] David Courtwright, *Dark Paradise: Opiate Addiction in America Before 1940* (Harvard Univ. Press, Cambridge MA 1982), p.105.

"Hasheesh, of which we know very little in this country, will doubtless be adopted by many of the unfortunates if they can get it."—Hamilton Wright, chief architect of US drug policy, July 25, 1909

California Origins of Cannabis Prohibition 49

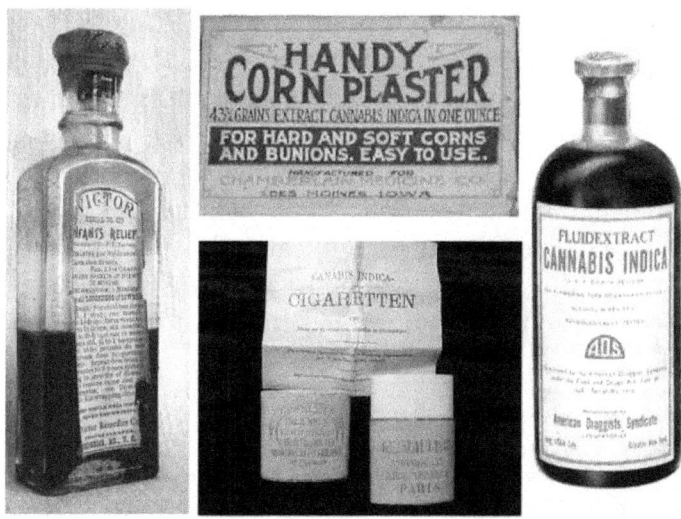

Cannabis remedies sold in drug stores (1840s–1910s)

Meanwhile, the issue was left to the states. Thence it was snatched up by a singular figure on the California State Board of Pharmacy, Henry J. Finger,[78] dubbed "the author of California's pharmacy law regulating sale of poisons."[79] An active figure in state Republican politics, Finger was one of the original appointees to the state's first board of pharmacy in 1891. He served until 1922,

---

[78] Henry James Finger (1853–1930) was born of German parents in San Francisco. After clerking in a Redwood City drugstore, he entered the first class of the California College of Pharmacy at the age of 17, but was unable to complete his studies due to lack of funds. In 1872 he repaired to Santa Barbara, where he established his own pharmacy business, catering to a large and growing clientele from 1875 to 1890. He was forced to discontinue the practice of pharmacy because of a "stubborn siege" of an unspecified chronic illness. Active in Republican politics, he served for three years as county coroner and public administrator. In 1891, he was appointed by Governor Markham to the first State Board of Pharmacy; six years later, he lost his seat when Governor Budd, a Democrat, replaced the Board, but he was re-appointed under the Republican administration of Governor Gage in 1901. Finger's retirement from active professional practice and support for aggressive enforcement made him unpopular among pharmacists. He showed a keen interest in having his expenses compensated, and was accused but exonerated of padding his expense account in a 1904 Board scandal. He was attentive to the ladies but opposed women's suffrage. He was a member of the Progressive Republicans, the Odd Fellows, and the Unitarian church. He retired from the Board in 1922. According to *Who's Who in California, 1928–29,* he authored "numerous papers and published addresses" on narcotics policy; unfortunately, he left no collected papers, and some of his writings appear to have been lost. Facts about Finger's early life are from James M. Guinn, *Historical and Biographical Record of Southern California* (Chapman Co., Chicago 1902).

[79] This epithet appears in *Who's Who in California, 1928–9*; similarly the *Pacific Drug Review* 27(12):26 (December 1915). However, it should be noted that Finger was absent from the board when the crucial 1907 poison amendments regarding narcotics were adopted.

taking a special interest in enforcement issues. Though a pharmacist by training, Finger became known as the "lawyer" of the board for his work in drafting legislation, such as the Itinerant Vendor Law against patent medicine peddlers (1903).[80] He lost his seat for one term due to a scandal in which he and other board members were accused by Hearst's *San Francisco Examiner* of irregularities and favoritism in licensing pharmacists.[81] Thanks to excellent political connections, he was reappointed by Governor Gillett in 1909. He became active on the board's Legal and Complaint Committee in charge of narcotics, where he championed vigorous and aggressive enforcement techniques.[82] Although highly unpopular with fellow pharmacists, Finger's efforts won favorable attention in higher circles. With a recommendation from Sen. Perkins and the brother of Secretary of State Philander Knox, he was appointed as one of three US delegates to the International Conference on Opium at the Hague in

---

[80] F.T. Herrick, "The Inebriate Law in Operation," *California Bulletin of Charities and Corrections* 1:11 (November 1911).

[81] An official investigation eventually exonerated the Board, but Governor Pardee declined to re-appoint the tainted members, specifically resisting repeated appeals to re-appoint Finger. Private communications in Finger's appointment file accuse him of dishonesty, favoritism and accepting money for pharmacy licenses: Governor George Pardee Papers, Appointment application letters, Box 3, Bancroft Library, U. California, Berkeley. The story of the scandal is told in the *San Francisco Examiner* August 17–24, 1904 and the *San Francisco Call* August 17–24 and December 30, 1904.

[82] "Hon. H.J. Finger Addresses V.C.P. Students on Harrison Act and State Poison Laws, February 13th," *The Drug Clerk's Journal* 7(6):20 (March 1918).

1911, along with Bishop Brent, the chief US delegate to the Shanghai Commission, and Hamilton Wright, who very much resented the appointment of the diplomatically inexperienced California pharmacist.[83]

An admitted greenhorn in international affairs, Finger consulted with Wright in preparation for the conference. Their correspondence, preserved in the National Archives, makes for interesting reading.[84] Aside from importuning Wright about arranging his itinerary to witness the coronation of George V in London, Finger offered to send Wright an opium outfit, seized in one of the Board's Chinatown forays, for display at the conference. Wright accepted this despite misgivings that any opium residue received therein would constitute a "highly punishable offense." On a similar note, Finger offered the conference a "very liberal supply" of "our very finest California wines" courtesy of Westmore and Co., who would be delighted at this fine opportunity to advertise their wares. This was too much for Wright, who called it "quite unbecoming an official delegate to have any understanding with any sort of producer" of the kind.

More importantly, Finger also had policy issues to discuss. Among these was the matter of Indian hemp, which Finger brought up in a curious letter to Wright dated July 2, 1911:

---

[83] Lowes, op. cit., pp. 170–4.

[84] Records of US Delegation to the International Opium Commission and Conferences of 1909–13, Record Group 43, Entry #40, Correspondence between Hamilton Wright and Henry J. Finger (National Archives).

Within the last year we in California have been getting a large influx of Hindoos and they have in turn started quite a demand for cannabis indica; they are a very undesirable lot and the habit is growing in California very fast; the fear is now that it is not being confined to the Hindoos alone but that they are initiating our whites into this habit.

We were not aware of the extent of this vice at the time our legislature was in session and did not have our laws amended to cover this matter, and now we have no legislative session for two years (January 1913).

This matter has been brought to my attention a great number of time[s] in the last two months and from the statements made to me by men of reliability it seems to be a real question that now confronts us; can we do anything in the Hague that might assist in curbing this matter?[85]

---

[85] Contrary to Professor David Musto's account in *The American Disease* (p. 218), there is nothing in Finger's letter to suggest that San Franciscans in particular were concerned by the threat. The overwhelming number of East Indians did not settle in the city, but in agricultural areas of the Central Valley: "California and the Oriental," Cal. State Board of Control, Report to Governor William Stephens, June 19, 1920; revised January 1, 1922: p. 122.

Henry J. Finger, the chair of the California Board of Pharmacy legal committee and proponent of the 1913 law against "Indian hemp"

The "Hindoos," actually East Indian immigrants of predominantly Sikh religion and Punjabi origin, had become a popular target of anti-immigrant sentiment after several boatloads arrived in San Francisco in 1910.[86] Their arrival sparked an uproar of protest from Asian exclusionists, who pronounced them to be even more unfit for American civilization than the Chinese. Their influx was promptly stanched by immigration authorities, leaving only about 2,600 in the state, mostly in agricultural areas of the Central Valley.[87] The "Hindoos" were widely denounced for their outlandish customs, dirty clothes, strange food, suspect morals, and especially their propensity to work for low wages. Some 90% of the "Hindoos" were Sikhs, who had initially come from British military service in China. The Sikhs were, by religion, opposed to smoking and the consumption of alcoholic beverages. On the other hand, Sikh soldiers were said by the British Indian Hemp Drugs Commission to be "extremely partial to *bhang*," a beverage concocted from hemp leaves.[88]

---

[86] On the East Indian immigration to California, see Jogesh C. Misrow, *East Indian Immigration on the Pacific Coast* (M.A. thesis, Stanford University, 1915); H.A. Millis, "East Indian Immigration to the Pacific Coast," *The Survey* 28:379–86 (June 1, 1912); Rajani Kanta Das, *Hindustani Workers on the Pacific Coast* (W. de Gruyter & Co., Berlin, 1923); and H. Brett Melendy, *Asians in America* (Twayne Publishing, Boston, 1977).

[87] Cal. State Board of Control, "California and the Oriental" (1922) p.122.

[88] *Report of the Indian Hemp Drugs Commission, 1893–94*, Ch. VIII, Section 410, p.152.

Finger's allegations about "Hindoo" cannabis use are confirmed by the remarks of a rubber planter from British Honduras who was interviewed by the *New York Sun* in a story republished by numerous newspapers in California and elsewhere.[89] "In California and down through Central America and the West Indies the practice of smoking ganjah, or Indian hemp, has been introduced within recent years... When the East Indian laborer was introduced into the West Indies about thirty years ago [i.e. 1880] he brought it with him... More recently, he did the same evil turn for California, so that at the present time ganjah smoking is prevalent from the Canadian border to Panama." Like contemporary accounts of marihuana, the article goes on to assert that ganjah renders smokers quarrelsome, bloodthirsty, and likely to commit murder. However, it fails to cite any specific instances of "Hindoo" ganjah use in California.

The article elicited editorial comments from the Temperance Department of the *Santa Cruz Sentinel* along the familiar lines of prohibitionists of the era:[90] "China has pointed out the proper method of dealing with ganjah. She prohibits the growth of

---

[89] "Ganja Smoking: Evils of a Practice Hindus Have Brought in the West Indies," *The Sun*, 13 March 1910, Third Section p. 5. The article was reprinted under various headings by the San Francisco *Bulletin* ("Ganjah Smoking Makes Murderers," 30 March 1910, p. 7), *Santa Cruz Sentinel* ("Introduction of Indian Hemp," 10 April 1910, p. 6); *Fresno Evening Herald*, ("Strange Story of Cannabis Smoking in State," 25 March 1910 editorial page), *Placer Herald* ("Ganjah Smoking a Curse," 21 March 1910 p.6), Arizona *Republic* ("Ganjah Smoking," 26 March 1910 p.7), *Detroit Free Press* ("Ganjah Smoking Spreads" 13 March 1910 p. 53) et. al.

[90] W.D. Storey, "Temperance Department," *Santa Cruz Sentinel*, 21 April 1910, p.6.

poppies from which opium is produced. Will Uncle Sam forbid the growth of ganjah? Will he interfere with the sacred personal liberty of the citizen to smoke the infernal weed? If he does, he will logically follow the course upon which he has already entered by prohibiting the importation and smoking of opium. And if our respected Uncle Sam does these things, who is going to complain? Why of course the brewers and distillers and big liquor dealers and little saoloonkeepers, will get upon their legs and rend the welkin with howls about the violation of their 'American liberty' and fanatical interference with their personal liberty. Nobody else will complain if Uncle Sam stamps out and utterly exterminates this vile twin of vile alcohol." Such indeed would be the case when the Board of Pharmacy moved to outlaw Indian hemp.

However, the ganjah issue was obscure enough not to further tarnish the image of "Hindoos" in California. Hindu immigrants were praised by employers as "temperate" and "the most sober of races."[91] "The taking of drugs as a habit scarcely exists among them," stated one sympathetic observer, a surprising fact given that many had resided in China and West Coast Chinatowns where opium use was rampant.[92]

At the insistence of California exclusionists, the Congress held hearings on Hindu immigration,

---

[91] Jogesh Misrow, *op. cit.*, p. 14.

[92] Rajani Kanta Das, *op. cit.*, p. 82.

where the question of drug use was raised briefly once and dismissed:[93]

> Rep. Manahan: Are they addicted to any kind of intoxication or drugs?
> Mrs. R.F. Patterson: I know that they do not drink. They do not indulge in drink. I don't know anything about their habits; no morphine, for instance; not to my knowledge.[94]

The committee did not pursue the drug issue further. Nonetheless, Finger's concerns were sympathetically received by Wright, who replied:

> I anticipated some time ago that in event of our securing Federal control of the sale and distribution of morphine and cocaine, the fiends would turn to Indian hemp, and for that reason incorporated that drug in the proposed act for the control of the interstate traffic in narcotics. In addition to this use by Hindus in this country, I have learned on good authority that it is commonly used by the Syrian element in our population. You certainly should have your legislature do something in regard to the control of Indian hemp. The Conference will deal with it, for the

---

[93] *Hindu Immigration,* hearings of the House Committee on Immigration relative to restrictions of immigration of Hindu laborers, 63rd Congress, 2nd Session, Part I: February 13, 1914, p. 22.

[94] Mrs. Patterson had resided for ten years in Calcutta, a center of Indian ganja culture, but had apparently not been impressed by a problem. Calcutta had the highest rate of ganja usage in India, amounting to 5.4% of the population, according to the Report of the Indian Hemp Drugs Commission: Ch. VIII, pp. 128–131.

Italian Government has informed us that it will bring the matter up in the Conference.[95]

It came to pass that the Italians dropped out of the conference, so the discussion of cannabis was deferred to a later date. However, the wheels were set in motion for legislation in California. At the next legislative session (1913), two companion bills to ban "narcotic preparations of hemp" were introduced by Assemblyman W.A. Sutherland of Fresno and Sen. Edward K. Strobridge of Hayward. [96]

By this time, another threat had appeared on the horizon: Mexican "marihuana" had begun to penetrate California. Marijuana (as it is now usually spelled[97]) was brought by Mexican immigrants, who arrived in mounting numbers during the revolutionary disorders of 1910-20.[98] An alert inspector of the state board of pharmacy took note and sounded the alarm in the *LA Times* shortly after

---

[95] Letter from Wright to Finger, July 11, 1911: National Archives, loc. cit.

[96] The bills were AB 907 and SB 630, respectively. They also included some technical revisions increasing penalties and clarifying the Board's enforcement powers. SB 630 was dropped and AB 907 passed into law.

[97] The spelling "marijuana" is not found in the earliest sources, but begins to appear in the 1920s: e.g. "Marijuana Seller Jailed," *Los Angeles Times,* November 15, 1923, p. 17.

[98] Marihuana is said to have arrived not only across the border from Mexico but also from the Caribbean into New Orleans around 1910. Frank B. Gomila, "Present Status of the Marihuana Vice in the US " in Robert P Walton, op. cit.

Finger and Wright had begun planning to legislate against Indian hemp.[99]

> In view of the increasing use of marihuano [sic] or loco weed as an intoxicant among a large class of Mexican laborers, F.C. Boden, inspector of the State Board of Pharmacy, yesterday formulated an appeal to the State authorities asking that the drug be included in the list of prohibited narcotics.
>
> For some undefined reason, the inspector asserts, the traffic in marihuano was not placed under the ban at the time the State law was passed forbidding the sale and possession of opiates and other drug intoxicants and if the present plans of the authorities are carried into effect, a determined campaign against the use of the deadly weed will at once be inaugurated.
>
> To this end the law now in force in Mexico will be copied and the possession, sale or use of the drug will be made a penal offense in California, if Boden's recommendations go through...
>
> If placed under the ban on equal terms with opiates it is believed the traffic in the drug can be much diminished, although it is considered an impossibility that it can be stamped out.

---

[99] "Would Prohibit Sale of Weed: State inspector would make it a penal offense," Los Angeles Times, October 10, 1911 p. II–5.

The Board's campaign was publicized nationally in a fanciful report that appeared in the *Washington Post, American Practitioner,* and *Pacific Medical Journal*:[100]

> "The Loco Weed": It is reported that the Mexican Marihuano or loco weed (*Astragalus hornu* [sic]) is being feared and fought by the California Board of Pharmacy as an enemy no less dreadful than opium or cocaine. This pernicious growth is of the hemp family, and grows up to six feet or more. The leaves yield under high pressure a kind of oil containing the narcotic principle; those of the male plant are preferred because they appear to contain a higher percentage of the narcotic than the leaves of the female plant. Several years ago this plant became so great a public menace in Mexico that drastic laws were passed to govern the production, sale and use of the narcotic; whilst these laws have had some good effect, more than one-third of the people of Mexico are believed to be more or less addicted to the use of the drug. Much of it is brought into California by the Mexican laborers, who are greatly addicted to it... [T]he loco narcotic destroys body, soul and

---

[100] The article was printed in the *Washington Post*, November 6, 1911, under the title "War on Crazing Drug: California Fears the Dread Loco Weed That Has Menaced Mexico," with a dateline reading "San Diego, Correspondence New York Sun." "The Loco Weed," *Pacific Medical Journal* 56:52 (January 1913), reprinted from *American Practitioner* 46:182–3 (April 1912).

mind. Its immediate effects are said to be a highly exhausted mental state of much longer continuance than that produced by morphine, and followed by sudden collapse. The hasheesh of India (*Cannabis Indica*) is almost like the Mexican drug plant. The common American loco weed, so troublesome to stockmen in the Southwest, is another variety, containing its own share of the narcotic principle... It is against the Mexican marihuano (an Indian name) that the fight is being waged, in order to have the prepared drug placed in the list of proscribed narcotics, making its sale, use, or possession a misdemeanor, punishable by heavy fine or imprisonment or both. It is purposed to copy the Mexican antiloco laws almost word for word into the California Penal Code.

The article is badly confused on the pharmacological and botanical identity of marihuana, which have nothing to do with *Astragalus hornii* or rancher's loco-weed. The female, not male parts of the plant are valued for being most potent. The claim that the Board dreaded "loco-weed" as much as opium or cocaine is suspect, given that the Board did not mention loco-weed, marijuana, or hashish in its biannual reports or minutes. Nor was the California legislation copied from Mexican "antiloco" laws.[101] Insofar as the Board

---

[101] Mexico's federal law prohibiting marijuana was not passed until 1920 ("Diario Oficial," March 15, 1920). Prior to that, there were sundry state laws and other control efforts dating back as far as 1855. Montfort, op. cit., p. 186.

had already been planning a law against Indian hemp for the reasons set forth by Finger and Wright, it seems likely that the new menace was incorporated by simply adding "loco-weed" to the text.

The details of the Board's deliberations are obscure. Like other narcotics legislation, the 1913 law received no press coverage and only the most cursory mention in pharmacy journals. The only published comment from the Board came from Finger's colleague C.B. Whilden, who cryptically remarked that legislation was needed "because of the increase in the use of 'hasheesh,' a detrimental preparation of hemp."[102]

Significantly, the Board's proposed anti-cannabis legislation was opposed by the pharmacy profession. In a poll by the California Pharmaceutical Association (CPhA), druggists voted by more than 2–1 that the "Poison Law should be left as it is." [103] Although the CPhA had originally been a close ally of the Board in the fight for "progressive" pharmacy legislation, it had become alienated by the Board's high-handed maneuvering in a dispute over a bill to

---

[102] *Pacific Drug Review* 25(3):89 (March 1913).

[103] The vote was 118 to 45: *Drug Clerk's Journal* 2(3): 32 (December 1912). There were "a few favoring a change whereby the trade would be allowed to sell carbolic acid full strength if properly registered, and still others favoring the restriction of cannabis indica, contending that its sale should be restricted to the same extent that cocaine and morphine are": *Pacific Drug Review* 25(1): 8 (January 1913).

tighten licensing requirements for pharmacists.[104] The Retail Druggists' Association of San Francisco put itself formally on record against the Board's proposed anti-cannabis legislation.[105] However, the Board was in firm control of the legislature, which passed it unanimously.

The new law, which took effect on August 10, 1913, had peculiar language. Rather than listing cannabis along with opiates and cocaine in Section 8 of the Poison Law, which governed the sale and possession of narcotics, the law took the curious form of an amendment to Section 8(a) concerning the possession of opium paraphernalia:

> Chapter 342 (1913) "Section 8(a). The possession of a pipe or pipes used for smoking opium (commonly known as opium pipes) or the usual attachment or attachments thereto, or **extracts, tinctures, or other narcotic preparations of hemp, or loco-weed, their preparations or compounds (except corn remedies containing not more than fifteen grains of the extract or fluid extract of hemp**

---

[104] The Board, led by Finger, scuttled a proposal by the CPhA to require a college degree of pharmacists. Finger's position is understandable in that he himself had been forced to drop out of the California College of Pharmacy due to financial problems. However, his role in this and other disputes left him highly unpopular with colleagues: *Pacific Pharmacist* 5:13 (May 1911) and *Pacific Drug Review* 23(4):9 (April, 1911). In a poll of over 100 pharmacists by the *Pacific Pharmacist*, no more than two (and possibly none) favored Finger for appointment to the Board; nonetheless, he was re-appointed by Governor Johnson: "The Pacific Pharmacist's Referendum Vote on Board Membership Qualifications," *Pacific Pharmacist* 6: 189–90 (December 1912).

[105] *Pacific Pharmacist* 6: 279 (March 1913).

to the ounce, mixed with not less than five times its weight of salicylic acid combined with collodion), is hereby made a misdemeanor..."

While the law was intended to restrict recreational use of hemp drugs, its language had unfortunate implications for pharmaceutical uses as well. The exemption for corn remedies protected what was then the most familiar (if medically dubious[106]) therapeutic use of cannabis by proprietary drug manufacturers.[107] However, cannabis was also used in proprietary remedies for cough, colic, and asthma and other prescription applications,[108] possession of which was outlawed

---

[106] Question: "In a corn cure composed of salicylic acid, extract of Indian hemp and collodion, what is the use of hemp?" Answer: "If we were facetiously inclined we might answer, 'to make a rope to hang the corn.' Seriously, the object of adding extract of *Cannabis indica* is something of a mystery. The person who originally devised the formula may have fancied that the extract would exert a sedative action and deaden the pain caused by the salicylic acid, but it is just as likely that it was a nice color he was after." *American Druggist* 45:8 (1904).

[107] Cannabis "is used almost altogether for the manufacture of corn cures and in veterinary practice," testified Albert Plaut, representing the pharmaceutical firm of Lehn & Fink, concerning Wright's proposed inclusion of cannabis in federal anti-narcotics legislation: *Importation and Use of Opium,* hearings before the House Committee on Ways and Means, 61st Congress, 3rd Session, January 11, 1911, p.75.

[108] A survey of 1108 patent medicines found cannabis in just two corn remedies and one cough remedy: "Report of the Commission on Proprietary Medicines of the American Pharmaceutical Association," *Journal of the APhA* 4: 1163 (1915). Other cannabis-containing medicines not mentioned in the APhA report included International Colic Remedy, Pratts Colic Remedy, and Chinatrocin

under the law. Taken literally, therefore, the law prohibited not only hashish, but almost all pharmaceutical hemp drugs.

In practice, there is no evidence that the law was ever used or intended to restrict pharmaceutical hemp drugs. Rather, it appears to have been misworded in a legislative blunder. Its language regarding hemp drugs would have made perfect sense had it been inserted in Section 8, restricting the sale and possession of other narcotics, as would have seemed logical in the first place. The effect of this would have been to outlaw the sale or possession of hemp drugs *without a prescription,* except for corn remedies, which had negligible potency. Such an exemption would have paralleled similar provisions in Section 8, exempting low-potency opiate and cocaine formulations from the prescription requirement. Unfortunately, this language made poor sense when inserted into the paraphernalia law, Section 8(a), since the latter did not allow for prescription distribution but rather banned possession absolutely.

It seems likely that the cannabis law was originally conceived as an amendment to Section 8, then carelessly moved to Section 8(a). This theory is supported by the fact that pharmacy journals erroneously reported that the law treated hemp drugs like other narcotics, as if they were actually in Section 8. The fact that the pharmacy journals never

---

Asthma Spray ("New Remedies of 1910–11," *San Francisco and Pacific Druggist* 16(5):11, January 1912).

explained the 1913 law accurately indicates just how obscure the cannabis issue was.[109]

How then did the cannabis law end up in Section 8(a)? Perhaps it was just the result of a clerical error, the substitution of 8(a) for 8. Alternatively, the law may have been deliberately recast as a paraphernalia provision on the theory that hemp intoxicants, like opium pipes, were more closely associated with street users than with pharmacies. As we shall see, there is evidence that the Mexicans, like the Syrians, grew their own marijuana, and the Hindus, being agricultural workers, would no doubt have been similarly inclined. This being so, it might have seemed silly to list cannabis in Section 8, which was designed to restrict sales by pharmacies. After all, why force pharmacies to maintain detailed records of their cannabis transactions when they weren't the source of the problem? By placing hemp drugs in Section 8(a), police could arrest errant hemp-heads, while leaving pharmacies free of unnecessary regulation.

In fact, there is evidence that pharmaceutical cannabis was occasionally diverted into recreational use in California. An investigation by the US Department of Agriculture of pharmacists along the Mexican border heard testimony that crude

---

[109] In an untypical journalistic error, the *Pacific Drug Review* 25(7):22 (July 1913) reported that the new law treated cannabis with "all provisions and penalties applying to it as now apply to the traffic in opium, morphine, cocaine, etc." The same error was repeated in the coverage of SB 630, an identical companion bill, by both *the Pacific Drug Review* 25(3):89 (March 1913) and the *Drug Clerk's Journal* 2(5):12 (February 1913).

medicinal *Cannabis indica* was sold to customers in Texas and other states, including California, for apparently non-medical purposes. [110]

This loophole was eliminated in 1915 when California's cannabis law was revised as part of a new package of technical amendments proposed by the Board of Pharmacy.[111] The new law listed cannabis alongside opium, morphine, cocaine, and chloral hydrate in Section 8 of the Poison Law. Specifically, it forbade the sale or possession of "flowering tops and leaves, extracts, tinctures and other narcotic preparations of hemp or loco weed *(Cannabis sativa)*, Indian hemp" except on prescription.[112] Even though Section 8 permitted the possession of legally prescribed narcotics, the possession of hemp drugs other than corn remedies remained independently outlawed under the 1913 paraphernalia provision, which remained on the books until 1937. Thus, *hemp pharmaceuticals remained technically legal to sell, but not possess, on prescription.* There are no grounds to believe that this prohibition was ever enforced, as hemp drugs

---

[110] 1917 Report to the US Department of Agriculture Bureau of Chemistry of investigations by R.F. Smith in the State of Texas, particularly along the Mexican border, of the traffic in and consumption of the drug known as "Indian Hemp," [photocopy from University of Virginia Law Library] pp. 12, 54, 73.

[111] State Senate Bill 1120 (Crowley). The most controversial provisions in the bill concerned restrictions on the sale of paregoric and corrosive sublimate of mercury: *San Francisco and Pacific Druggist* 19(7): 17 (March 1915).

[112] Statutes of California, Chapter 604 (1915).

continued to be prescribed in California for years to come.[113]

Like its predecessor, the 1915 cannabis law received no attention at the time.[114] Later, it would be recorded by drug historians—incorrectly—as the state's first anti-cannabis law.[115] The 1913 law was undoubtedly overlooked because it was an amendment to the obscure paraphernalia law. Moreover, of course, the cannabis problem was itself still obscure, so much so that even its original discoverer soon forgot about it when, in a 1917 lecture, Finger declared that the only difference between the Harrison Act and California's pharmacy law was that the latter also restricted chloral

---

[113] Records from Wakelee's Pharmacy in San Francisco show three prescriptions containing cannabis among 300 prescriptions in November 1907, and one cannabis prescription among 300 in December 1917 (in the California Historical Society, San Francisco).

[114] The *Sacramento Bee* briefly noted that a bill was passed "making more difficult the obtainment of drugs or narcotics by fiends" (March 24, 1915, p.5). The *San Francisco Examiner* (March 24) and *Los Angeles Examiner* (March 25) mentioned only the bill's more controversial provisions concerning the sale of paregoric and corrosive sublimate of mercury.

[115] The 1915 date is given by Morgan, *op. cit.;* Bonnie & Whitebread, *The Marihuana Conviction: A History of Marihuana Prohibition in the United States* (University of Virginia, Charlottesville 1974) p. 354; Ron Hamowy, *Dealing With Drugs* (Lexington Books, Lexington MA 1987) pp. 10–11; and California Attorney General Evelle Younger, "The Development of California's Drug Law: An Historical Perspective," *Journal of Drug Issues* 8(3): 263–70 (Summer 1978). A likely source of the error is the Surgeon General's report, "State Laws Relating to the Control of Narcotic Drugs and the Treatment of Drug Addiction," Supplement #91 to the Public Health Reports (1931), p. 48.

hydrate—forgetting entirely about *Cannabis indica*.[116]

In sum, it appears that cannabis-using Hindoos and Mexicans were merely a handy excuse for the Board to work its will. In the political climate of the era, no further excuse was needed. The early 1910s marked the high tide of progressivism in California when public opinion supported government regulation of social purity. The same decade saw the culmination of the alcohol prohibition movement, which secured passage of the 18th Amendment in 1919. Although Californians were resistant to "bone-dry" prohibition, many of them, including Finger and his colleagues in the pharmacy profession, favored wine and beer as healthful "temperance" beverages[117] and there was broad agreement on the evils of hard liquor and intoxication in general.[118] In 1914 and 1916, prohibition initiatives made the state ballot. Meanwhile, the legislature was tackling such moral issues as prostitution, racetrack gambling, prizefighting, and liquor zoning, not to mention oral

---

[116] H.J. Finger, "Law and Pharmacy," *The Pacific Pharmacist* 11:30 (May 1917).

[117] Like many of his colleagues in the California pharmacy profession, Finger was of German parentage, an ethnic group that opposed prohibition of beer and wine. Thus the *Pacific Pharmacist*, edited by Albert Schneider, condemned the saloon but judged wine to be a "wholly ethical business": *Pacific Pharmacist* 8:71 (August 1914).

[118] On the politics of alcohol prohibition in California, see Gilman M. Ostrander, *The Prohibition Movement in California, 1848–1933* (University of California, Berkeley 1957).

sex.[119] Amidst this profusion of vices, Indian hemp was but a minor afterthought.

---

[119] Franklin Hichborn chronicled the proceedings of the Progressive era legislatures, including that of 1913, with some attention to alcohol and morals issues, but never mentioned narcotics: *Story of The California Legislature 1909; 1911; 1913; 1915* (James H. Barry Co., San Francisco, 1909–15).

The First Marijuana Busts

Although the passage of the law attracted no notice, the Board's enforcement efforts soon brought marijuana to public attention in Los Angeles, where the Board's agents launched a crackdown in the city's Mexican Sonoratown neighborhood in 1914. In what may be the first US newspaper account of a marijuana cultivation bust, the *Los Angeles Times* reported that two "dream gardens" containing $500 worth of Indian hemp or "marahuana" had been eradicated by Board Inspector Roy Jones.[120] The paper explained:

> Indian hemp is a plant having potent narcotic properties and was blacklisted under the poison law in the last Legislature. Surrounding it are sinister legends of murder, suicide and disaster... According to Inspector Jones and Detectives Leon and Rico, well

---

[120] "Wagonload of Dreams Seized," *Los Angeles Times*, September 10, 1914, p.2. A possession case, in which an alleged "Mexican drug vendor" named R. Franks received a stiff sentence of six months and $250, was reported the previous day in the *Los Angeles Examiner*, September 9, 1914, p.1. According to a brief *Times* report a week earlier, busts of "several wagon loads" had already occurred: "Confiscate Hemp," *LA Times*, September 3, 1914, p. II 8.

acquainted with Sonoratown life, the weed is much used in the local Mexican colony. In out-of-the-way nooks and corners small plants are nursed and often provide the bare livelihood of the cultivators.

According to the *Los Angeles Examiner,* it was police who "surrounded marihuana with a legend of murder and crime."[121]

The *Times* furnished further details in a pair of marijuana bust stories published three weeks later:

> Several years ago a number of Mexicans living on the east side made an industry of raising the Indian hemp, planning to get rich quick... Recently the tendency to use the stuff has reached alarming proportions, and it is the intention of the Marshal and other officials to adopt strong measures, if necessary, to stamp out the vice.[122]

A local police judge expressed similar views when, having previously heard two Mexican defendants charged with assault plead that they had been under the influence of marijuana, he handed down a tough, six-month sentence to another

---

[121] "Marihuana Growers Placed Under Arrest," *Los Angeles Examiner*, September 10, 1914, II-1.

[122] "Police Stop Sales of Drug in Tobacco Bags," *Los Angeles Times*, September 30, 1914, II–8.

defendant arrested with enough marijuana to make 1,000 cigarettes: [123]

> The habit of taking this drug is increasing with such alarming rapidity that it is becoming one of the most menacing problems in police work... More men are seriously injured by persons under the influence of marahuana tha[n] from any two causes.

Evidently, there was an incipient interest in suppressing marijuana in law enforcement circles, despite a lack of apparent broader public concern.

The Board capped its kick-off campaign with a dramatic flourish by burning one ton of marihuana along with confiscated opium, cocaine, and paraphernalia in a public bonfire at the Plaza in Los Angeles. [124]

The *Los Angeles Times* ran the best early coverage about marihuana in the period before 1920. Included was an account of the state's first medical marijuana arrestee, a Mexican maid who insisted that she was raising marijuana tea for stomach trouble.[125] The maid was arrested under an Orange County ordinance that made it a

---

[123] "High Cost of Dope Smoking," *Los Angeles Times*, September 27, 1914, II–2.

[124] "Drugs to Rise Like Incense," *Los Angeles Times*, October 16, 1914, II–1; "In Fanciful Forms Contraband Goes Up," *Los Angeles Times*, October 17, 1914, II–5.

[125] "Officers Object to 'Dream Weed' Crop," *Los Angeles Times*, July 6, 1919, V-9.

misdemeanor to possess or cultivate marijuana.[126] This ordinance (fittingly from a county whose sheriff led the opposition to California's 1996 medical marijuana initiative) is the earliest evidence of local government interest in joining the Board's anti-cannabis efforts.

Meanwhile, in Northern California, marijuana remained undiscovered. As late as 1920, an exposé of the San Francisco drug scene, *The Hop-heads,* by journalist Fred Williams, portrayed vices ranging from morphine and cocaine to tobacco and prostitution but failed to mention marijuana.[127] Sacramento police arrest logs from the era mention opium, morphine, cocaine, yen shee, and opium pipes, but not Indian hemp or loco-weed.[128] Not until 1921 did the *San Francisco Examiner* mention that "Mexican hasheesh" or "marihuana" was being smuggled into the Presidio army base by unknown culprits.[129] Two years later, "marihuana" made its

---

[126] The ordinance was passed two years previously, about 1917. In a pattern prefiguring modern medical marijuana cases, the woman, who had been growing a dozen plants, two of them over 14 feet tall, was rebuked by the judge, who declared, "That stuff isn't growing for stomach, but for your head." *Santa Ana Daily Register*, July 7, 1919, p.3.

[127] Fred V. Williams, *The Hop-heads: personal experiences among the users of "dope" in the San Francisco underworld* (W.W. Brunt, San Francisco, 1920).

[128] Sacramento Jail Register, Record of Arrests, 1913–1916 et al., Sacramento Archives.

[129] "Presidio Peril Feared; Hunt for Hasheesh," *San Francisco Examiner,* August 7, 1921, p.3.

début in the *New York Times*.[130] By 1924, arrests were being reported in Sacramento.[131]

Other states passed laws against cannabis before World War I: Massachusetts in 1911;[132] Maine, Wyoming, and Indiana in 1913; and Utah[133] and Vermont in 1915.[134] City ordinances were also

---

[130] "Marihuana is newest drug," *New York Times*, January 11, 1923, p 24. Prior to this, New York City was said to be experiencing an upsurge in "hasheesh," originally introduced by the Turks and Armenians, but also used in the "Spanish section" and Greenwich Village, according to a report in the *San Francisco Examiner* (April 10, 1921). Note that New York City had already banned cannabis in 1914.

[131] "City News in Brief," *Sacramento Bee,* November 12, 1924 p. 5; ibid., July 15, 1925, p.5.

[132] Early cannabis laws in Massachusetts, Maine and Vermont were the work of anti-vice crusader Henry Chase: George Fisher, "Racial Myths of the Drug War," *Boston University Law Review* v. 101:933 (2021). *Cannabis indica* and sativa were first mentioned in Massachusetts pharmacy law in 1911 (Chapter 372) and 1912 (Chapter, 283).

[133] According to Professor Charles Whitebread, the Utah law was enacted pursuant to the condemnation of marihuana in August, 1915 by the Church of Jesus Christ of Latter-day Saints (Mormon church), which had learned of the vice from a band of Mormon colonists returning from Mexico. Before that, however, the Utah Board of Pharmacy had requested the California Board of Pharmacy to send a copy of the state's 1915 pharmacy amendments—which included the provision against cannabis—saying that Utah wished to adopt the California law: Minutes of the Cal. Board of Pharmacy, February 2, 1915 (State Archives, Sacramento); cf. Charles Whitebread, "The History of the Non-Medical Use of Drugs in the United States," Speech to the 1995 California Judges Association annual conference, posted at www.druglibrary.org/schaffer/ History/HISTORY.HTM.

[134] Compilations of early cannabis laws appear in Bonnie & Whitebread, *The Marihuana Conviction*, p. 354, and Hamowy, op. cit., pp. 10–11. The latter corrects several inaccuracies and omissions in the former for the period before 1930, but both miss California's 1913 and Massachusetts' 1911 laws.

enacted in New York City in 1914[135] and Portland, Oregon, in 1915.[136] As in California, these early laws were passed not in response to any public outcry but as preventative initiatives by drug control authorities to deter future use.

On New Year's Day, 1913, El Paso, Texas became the scene of the nation's first public marijuana scare when a Mexican desperado, allegedly crazed by habitual marijuana use, ran amok and killed a policeman, generating front-page news in the *El Paso Herald*.[137] This inspired a grand jury investigation, which prompted the city to ban marijuana in 1915.[138] Like California's 1913 law, the El Paso ordinance accidentally banned medical uses

---

[135] The New York ordinance was promulgated by the City Board of Health: *New York Times*, July 29, 1914, p.6, cited in Richard Bonnie & Charles Whitebread, "The Forbidden Fruit and the Tree of Knowledge: An Inquiry into the Legal History of American Marijuana Prohibition," *Virginia Law Review* 56(6), October 1970.

[136] The Portland law stemmed from an incident in which a group of young boys were observed procuring cannabis unchecked at local pharmacies. The city fathers responded by restricting cannabis sales to prescription only. This appears to be the first instance of a law inspired specifically by youthful cannabis use. *Pacific Drug Review*, 27(4): 65 (April 1915) and 27(7):26 (July 1915).

[137] "Crazed by a Weed, Man Murders," *El Paso Herald*, January 2, 1913 p. 1.

[138] The date of the El Paso ordinance is misreported as 1914 by Bonnie & Whitebread (pp. 33–34), evidently based on an erroneous statement in the 1917 Report to the US Department of Agriculture Bureau of Chemistry ("Investigations by R.F. Smith in the State of Texas," p.9). In reality, the law took effect on June 14, 1915: "Grand Jury Recommends that Steps be Taken to Stop Sale of Marihuana," *El Paso Herald*, October 4, 1913, p. 2; "Marihuana Sale Now Prohibited," *El Paso Herald*, June 3, 1915, p.6; "New Anti-Marihuana Ordinance Very Stringent," *El Paso Herald*, June 7, 1915, p.9.

of cannabis as well.[139] In response to the El Paso ordinance, the US Department of the Treasury issued an order banning importation of cannabis for non-medical purposes in 1915.[140] However, this was academic insofar as users had largely relied on pharmaceutical supplies or else grown their own domestically.

The 1920s saw a widening, though still quite sporadic, interest in marihuana, usage of which may have been encouraged by the lack of alcohol during Prohibition. During this period, the press devoted increasing attention to the "dope menace." In an early installment of the Hearst papers' decades-long crusade against drugs, the *Los Angeles Examiner* ran a front-page picture of a "cigaret of poisonous marihuana or Mexican 'crazy' weed" along with morphine injection paraphernalia.[141] In what would become a classic line, the *Examiner* quoted a young peddler from Long Beach saying, "Marahuana's a Mexican weed that many of 'em begin on. I got my start with marahuana." [142] The *Los Angeles Times* followed up with a droll story, "Happy daffodils grow

---

[139] "While the ordinance is designed to avoid the sale of this drug for smoking purposes, no mention is made in the new law that it may be used legitimately. Nearly all the drug stores in the city have quantities on hand for use in prescriptions, though they say they never sell it to smokers. The published ordinance will make it a felony for drug stores to have this drug on hand." *El Paso Herald*, June 7, 1915, p.9.

[140] Treasury Decision 35719, Sept. 25, 1915: Bonnie & Whitebread, p. 53.

[141] "5,000 Addicts Roam City Begging Dope! Startling Increase of Drug Slaves Greatest Menace to Community," *Los Angeles Examiner*, October 13, 1921, p. 1.

[142] *Los Angeles Examiner*, September 19, 1920, p.3.

on bird seed plant," subtitled, "Hemp leaf turned into marihuana causes smoker to become madman and run amuck."[143]

Press reports of marijuana remained highly sporadic throughout the 1920s. Not until 1928 did the *San Francisco Chronicle* first report a marijuana arrest.[144] Prior to this, its Hearst press rival provided occasional colorful nuggets of misinformation in the course of its ongoing anti-dope crusade. According to the *San Francisco Examiner*, marijuana cigarettes were a "short cut to the lunatic asylum" for adults and "sure death" for children.[145] In a prelude to the famous "Reefer Madness" campaign of the 1930s, Hearst's "sob sister" columnist, Annie Laurie (a.k.a. Winifred Black), warned that "Marihuana makes fiends of boys in 30 days."[146] Picking up on Mexican marijuana mythology, Laurie warned, "Hasheesh will turn the mildest man in the world into a bloodthirsty murderer. The man who takes hasheesh 'runs amuck' with his bloody knife in one hand and his strangling cloth in the other, and he kills, kills, kills, until the hasheesh has burnt out its deadly flame. Heroin is almost as bad."[147] Despite such comments,

---

[143] *Los Angeles Times*, April 30, 1922, II–10.

[144] "Two Jailed After Crazy Weed Find," September 28, 1928, p.5.

[145] Annie Laurie, "Report Bares Dope Problem Facing US," *San Francisco Examiner*, January 21, 1923, p. 12.

[146] *San Francisco Examiner*, January 31, 1923, p.11.

[147] "Heroin, Once Heralded as 'Safe,' Now Regarded as Worst 'Narcotic,' Drives Victims to Bold Crimes," *San Francisco Examiner*, February 27, 1927, p. 9.

the brunt of the Hearst press' anti-dope crusade was directed against opiates and cocaine.

As anti-narcotics sentiment hardened in California in the 1920s, so did penalties. Illegal sale, which had initially been a misdemeanor punishable by a $100–$400 fine and/or 50–180 days in jail for first offenders, became punishable by six months to six years in 1925. Possession, which had previously been treated the same as sales, became punishable by up to six years in prison. In 1927, the law against opium dens was finally extended to Indian hemp, as originally envisioned in the 1880 Walker bill. In 1929, second offenses for possession became punishable by sentences of six months–10 years.

Ironically, Henry Finger would probably have disapproved of such draconian prison terms. Finger had advocated that drug habitués be sent to state hospitals for treatment rather than confined in prison.[148] However, efforts to this end were frustrated by a lack of funds and political will. [149]

In a preview of things to come, the campaign against marijuana began to impinge on California's hemp fiber industry. In 1928, public hearings were

---

[148] Henry Finger, "Pharmaceutical Legislation in California—Inebriates and Drug Habitues Law," *Drug Clerk's Journal* 1(1):21 (October 1911).

[149] On the failure of California's efforts to establish a system of hospitals for inebriates, see Jim Baumohl and Sarah W. Tracy, "Building Systems to Manage Inebriates: The Divergent Paths of California and Massachusetts, 1891–1920," *Contemporary Drug Problems*, 21:557–97 (1994); and Jim Baumohl, "'Now We Won't Call It Lobbying: The Federal Bureau of Narcotics and the Depression-Era Maintenance Controversy in California and Washington," paper presented at Conference on Historical Perspectives on Alcohol and Drug Use in American Society, 1800–1997, College of Physicians, Philadelphia, May 9–11, 1997.

called by the state Commissioner of Corporations to determine whether the Imperial Linen Products Co. should be granted a corporate license to raise hemp in the Imperial Valley after officials raised public safety concerns that Mexican laborers might use the hemp for marijuana.[150] The company was supported by experts from the USDA Bureau of Plant Industry, who testified that there was no serious risk of narcotic production from hemp since it contained negligible quantities of the narcotic element in marijuana.[151] The license was granted on the unprecedented conditions that the company (1) notify the sheriff of each county where it intended to grow hemp and (2) cooperate at its own expense with law enforcement in policing the crop.[152] Later, after the passage of the Marihuana Tax Act, hemp agriculture in California was finally quashed by the Federal Bureau of Narcotics.[153]

---

[150] Letter to Dr. W.W. Stockberger, Bureau of Plant Industry, from Edward Cormack, Secretary of Imperial Linen Products Corp., January 27, 1928 (courtesy of John Lupien).

[151] "Hemp Problem Investigated by Commission," *Brawley News*, February 3, 1928, p.1; "Probe on Hemp Culture Opens at Court House," *Imperial Valley Press*, February 3, 1928, p.6.

[152] "Crazy Weed Precaution," *San Francisco Chronicle*, March 7, 1928, p.7.

[153] In 1940, federal agents seized a shipment of hemp stalks sent by the Amhempco Corp. of Illinois to Mr. Leland O. Walker, who had a hemp decorticating fibre machine in Chula Vista. FBN Commissioner Anslinger threatened to file charges and warned that future shipments would not be allowed. Three years later, FBN officials discouraged an application by Mr. John Laidlaw of Chicago to cultivate hemp in California, claiming that California law prohibited cultivation of cannabis. Thanks to John Lupien for documentation from his unpublished manuscript, "Hemp and

Despite heightened enforcement, marijuana use spread inexorably. The first official statistics on marijuana arrests date from 1925–6, when they accounted for one-quarter of drug arrests in Los Angeles and 4% of those in San Francisco.[154] According to the State Narcotic Committee, "In the northern part of the state, fully 85 percent of our arrests involve morphine, but in and around Los Angeles marihuana is so generally used by the Mexican addicts that only about 50 percent of the arrests there involve morphine." By 1930, marijuana had reached nearly 60% of arrests in Los Angeles and 26% statewide, in a year when there were 878 total narcotics arrests.

History's Future," including communications from Harry Anslinger, FBN District Supervisor Joseph Manning, FBN Deputy Commissioner Will S. Wood, John S. Laidlaw, et al.

[154] State Narcotic Committee, "Report on Drug Addiction in California," Sacramento, 1926, p. 14.

Marihuana plant showing seed. Photo by Joseph B. Swim.

Marihuana makes its debut in the State Narcotic Committee Report, "The Trend of Drug Addiction in California." 1931

Press interest in marijuana peaked in the early 30s. Marijuana briefly made lurid headlines in the *Los Angeles Examiner*, which proclaimed, "Marihuana Menaces Los Angeles School Children: Pupils Find Deadly Dope Easy to Get."[155] Simultaneously, in Sacramento, police declared a drive on marijuana, saying that scarcity of other narcotics had increased its use.[156] However, these scares were not long-lived.

The State Narcotic Committee took a calmer view of cannabis in its 1931 report, observing, "Fortunately, it will never be as serious a problem as the narcotic drugs, because it is not cumulative in its effect and the sudden discontinuance of its use produces no withdrawal symptoms." Two years later, when the Depression was causing pressure for budget cutbacks, state Narcotics Division chief William Walker warned that the state was "wide opened to the ravages of 'loco weed' with nothing to stop its use by 5 million persons." "The marihuana situation is more serious than anyone but the State knows," he went on. "Requests are pouring in from sheriffs, chiefs of police, and peace officers of all kinds, asking aid in running down growers and peddlers... Unless State aid is forthcoming, the situation will be wide open by the end of the year."[157] Later, however, after the agency's budget crisis was over, Walker's views on marijuana changed, and he came to oppose the proposed federal Marihuana Tax

---

[155] *Los Angeles Examiner*, February 18, 1930, p.1.

[156] "Drive on Marajuana [sic] in City is Planned," *Sacramento Bee*, February 21, 1930, p.9.

[157] *San Francisco Chronicle*, October 4, 1933 p.4; quoted in Morgan, op. cit., p. 145.

Act, probably out of concern over its unenforceability.[158]

By and large, California was unfazed by the famous Reefer Madness campaign of the later 1930s. The state having already outlawed the drug, the push for a federal law received little notice. US Commissioner of Narcotics Harry Anslinger singled out California for having exemplary narcotics laws that needed no amendment.[159] In 1937, the state did add cannabis cultivation as a separate offense. In the next legislature, for the first time, the word "marihuana" was written into the law when the narcotics code was rewritten as part of the new Health and Safety Code.[160]

Not until 1940 did the state finally publish a brief pamphlet, "Marihuana: Our Newest Narcotic Menace."[161] It reported, among other items:

> Up to about ten years ago... this dangerous drug was virtually unknown in the United States...
>
> Marihuana... is an excitant drug. It attacks the central nervous system and

---

[158] Jim Baumohl, "'Now We Won't Call It Lobbying," op. cit., and personal communication July 14, 1998.

[159] H.J. Anslinger, "The National Narcotic Situation," in the *Report on Drug Addiction in California* by the [State] Senate Interim Narcotic Committee (Sacramento, 1936), pp. 16–17.

[160] Statutes of California, 1939 Chapter 60.

[161] "Marihuana: Our Newest Narcotic Menace," Division of Narcotic Enforcement, Sacramento 1940. Walker was out of office by the time this pamphlet was written.

> violently affects the mentality and the five physical senses...
>
> Marihuana has no therapeutic or medicinal value that can not better be replaced by other drugs. It serves no legitimate purposes whatsoever...
>
> In 1937, the state confiscated 2,926,802 grains [418 lbs.], enough for 300,000 cigarettes...
>
> Fortunately, marihuana is not habit-forming to the extent that other drugs are... [W]hen deprived of his drug... the marihuana user will at most feel a mere hankering or craving much like the user of tobacco or alcohol. Considering the dangers involved, there can be no excuse for using or peddling marihuana: anyone guilty of either should be brought promptly to the most severe punishment provided by law.

Despite the state's best efforts, marijuana use spread inexorably beyond LA's Mexican community to jazz musicians, hipsters, the Black community, and Hollywood entertainers, many of whom were caught up in scandalous busts for personal use in the 1930s–1950s: Louis Armstrong and his drummer Vic Berton, Gene Krupa, Eddie Heywood, Anita O'Day, Robert Mitchum and Lila Leeds, and Rita Moreno.[162]

---

[162] For a detailed account of early marijuana busts in Los Angeles, see Sarah Brady Siff, "Targeted Marijuana Law Enforcement in Los Angeles, 1914–59," *Fordham Urban Law Journal* Vol. 49#3 (2022). Siff documents many Mexican arrests, which is natural since they

After taking a back seat to the war, anti-narcotics efforts intensified in the 1950s. Penalties for marijuana possession were hiked to a minimum of one to ten years in prison in 1954, and sale was made punishable by five to fifteen years with a mandatory three years before eligibility for parole. Two prior felonies raised the maximum sentences for both offenses to life.

None of this did anything to prevent a surge in marijuana use in the late 1950s. Arrests for marijuana soared from 140 in 1935 to 5,155 per year in 1960. Before long, the trend exploded into a mass phenomenon as pot-smoking hippies flocked to San Francisco to celebrate the Summer of Love.

For the first time in history, a ballot initiative to re-legalize personal use of marijuana was placed on the ballot by a volunteer coalition known as Amorphia in 1972. Although the California Marijuana Initiative lost 2–1 at the polls, it did better than expected, showing there existed a surprising constituency for marijuana. Meanwhile, by 1974, marijuana arrests skyrocketed to a record 103,097, almost all of them felonies.

Overwhelmed by law enforcement costs, the legislature passed the Moscone Act of 1975, ending criminal arrests and imprisonment for possession of one ounce or less. Arrests promptly plummeted to about half their previous level, most of them now misdemeanors instead of felonies. Nonetheless, state officials still struggled to suppress the illegal

---

became the chief suppliers of the drug, but dubiously ascribes "anti-Mexican aims" to California's original law against cannabis.

market, as cultivation and sales remained felony offenses, and California offered fertile grounds for a lucrative marijuana industry in its remote Emerald Triangle wilderness, where hundreds of millions of dollars' worth of plants were eradicated by the state's helicopter-led Campaign Against Marijuana Planting (CAMP).

In the meantime, a growing number of users were discovering the medicinal value of cannabis for the treatment of nausea and appetite loss due to cancer chemotherapy, neuropathy from HIV, glaucoma, and other conditions. With its politically active HIV community, San Francisco became the center of a new medical cannabis movement. Led by longtime pot dealer and gay activist Dennis Peron, petitioners placed a medical marijuana initiative, Proposition P, on the 1991 city ballot. Proposition P was approved by a whopping 79.4% of San Francisco voters, leading all other measures on the ballot. Although Proposition P was technically just a resolution and didn't change any laws, Peron soon set up the first "cannabis buyers club," openly selling cannabis to patients with a doctor's note of medical eligibility. The medical marijuana campaign soon spread statewide, and in 1996, California voters approved Proposition 215, legalizing both the possession and cultivation of marijuana for personal medical purposes. For the first time since 1913, cannabis could be legally grown and used in California (and for the first time since 1937 in the US). Proposition 215 proved to be a landmark in drug legislation, setting off a wave of similar medical marijuana measures in other states and foreign countries. Within a few years, hundreds of semi-licit patients' collectives were serving over a million users in California. However, there remained a larger, non-medical market, accounting for over 17,000 felonies and 60,000 misdemeanor arrests per year by 2008. Activists organized a new, adult use California legalization initiative, Proposition 19, in 2010, which, though falling short at the ballot, gained enough votes (46.5%) to inspire subsequent, successful legalization initiatives in Colorado and Washington in 2012. Finally, in 2016, California followed suit by approving another voter initiative, the Adult Use of Marijuana Act, Proposition 64, which legalized adult use under a system of state-licensed production, sales, and distribution.

Cartoon celebrating the federal prohibition on the medical use of marijuana. Published in *Pacific Drug Review*, November 1937

Prohibition a Bureaucratic Initiative

Cannabis was outlawed in California not in response to any perceived public outcry but as the result of a bureaucratic initiative by the State Board of Pharmacy. Unlike the prohibition of alcohol, opiates, and cocaine, the prohibition of cannabis was not accompanied by any widespread concern or awareness of problems surrounding its use. Prior to 1914, the recreational use of hemp drugs was largely unknown in California. Unlike the East Coast, California produced no known hashish literature, no medicinal cannabis research, and no tales of hashish dens. Nor was there any public alarm concerning cannabis use. Ironically, it was only after cannabis was outlawed in 1913 that stories of marijuana began to appear in the press, when the first enforcement measures were taken in the Mexican community of Los Angeles. The entirety of the modern "marijuana problem" arose after cannabis was prohibited.

The origins of cannabis prohibition in California defy the traditional explanation of marihuana prohibition, as related in the story of the federal Marihuana Tax Act of 1937. Unlike its federal successor, the 1913 law had nothing to do with the "Reefer Madness" campaign, the propaganda of William Randolph Hearst, or the bureaucratic machinations of Harry Anslinger. Still less was it due to a fanciful conspiracy of Hearst and DuPont to suppress industrial hemp, as proposed by some modern-day hempsters.[163] Neither can it be blamed on anti-Mexican hysteria: prejudice against Mexicans was not a significant factor in California politics until the 1920s, and even then, their use of "marihuana" attracted no notice.[164] Indeed, anti-

---

[163] This myth was widely popularized in the 1990 and subsequent editions of Jack Herer's underground classic, *The Emperor Wears No Clothes: Hemp and the Marijuana Conspiracy* (ed. Chris Conrad, HEMP Publishing, Van Nuys, CA), in Chapter 4 "The Last Days of Legal Cannabis." The story goes that Hearst and DuPont conspired to suppress industrial hemp because it competed with their manufacturing interests (Hearst's in wood-pulp-based paper, DuPont's in coal-and-oil-based plastics). Herer never produced an iota of evidence to substantiate this theory. To the contrary, according to Hearst's biographer, W.A. Swanberg, Hearst's newspaper empire was heavily dependent on imports of Canadian newsprint, rising prices of which left him seriously strapped for cash by 1939. It therefore seems that it would actually have been in Hearst's interest to promote cheap hemp paper substitutes, had that been a viable alternative. W.A. Swanberg, *Citizen Hearst* (Charles Scribner's Sons, New York, 1961), pp. 581–2.

[164] The thesis that opposition to marijuana was rooted in anti-Mexican sentiment is expounded by John Helmer in *Drugs and Minority Oppression* (Seabury Press, NY, 1975), Chapter 4, "Mexicans and Marijuana," but Helmer focuses on the period of the late 1920s and 30s, after the first laws were passed. An upsurge in Mexican immigration hit California around 1914, but labor shortages kept Mexicans in demand as agricultural workers through World War I, and not until the 1920s did their numbers inspire significant anti-Mexican sentiment: Matt Meier and Feliciano Ribera, *Mexican Americans/American Mexicans* (Farrar, Straus and Giroux, NY, 1993), pp. 111–26. Even then, neither anti-Mexican groups nor investigators concerned with Mexican labor and crime problems

Mexican tropes are notably lacking in the propaganda of the Reefer Madness era.[165] As noted by Professor Isaac Campos, the so-called "Mexican hypothesis" of marijuana prohibition was popularized by scholars in the 1970s, who argued that prejudice against Mexican immigrants and their supposed partiality to the marijuana habit led whites to unfairly demonize it, much like the Chinese and smoking opium.[166] However, as Campos points out, marijuana was little used by most Mexicans, and the drug's evil reputation for violence and madness actually originated in Mexico.

Nor, finally, was the 1913 law due to anti-Oriental sentiment, Finger's letter about "Hindoos" notwithstanding. The Hindus' hemp use was never widely known but was merely an excuse for Finger to act on his own prohibitionist instincts. Had the Hindus come to California in 1895, their cannabis use would have stirred up no more reaction than did the Syrians'.

What had changed in 1913 was the emergence of a new class of professional public policy bureaucrats with the authority and will to regulate drugs in California. This class, represented

---

ever mentioned their use of marihuana: Patricia Morgan, op. cit., pp. 73–91.

[165] In researching this history, the author was unable to find a single article, editorial, or cartoon in the Hearst press or other Reefer Madness literature, deprecating Mexicans for the use of marijuana. Neither did Helmer's analysis, based on economic and criminological data, cite any.

[166] Isaac Campos, "Mexicans and the Origins of Marijuana Prohibition in the United States: A Reassessment," *Social History of Alcohol and Drugs*, Vol. 32 (2108).

by Henry Finger and the State Board of Pharmacy, came to power with the Progressive Era revolution in government. Prompted by temperance sentiment and the rise of the worldwide anti-narcotics movement, the Board enlisted the legislature in a policy of narcotics prohibition in 1907. The inclusion of cannabis was but a logical extension based on prohibitionist principles. As argued by Patricia Morgan, "The first mention of cannabis in the California statutes should not be seen as moral reform, but rather as an example of professional reform policy tied to the overall ideology of the Progressive Era."[167]

The 1913 law was essentially preemptive, aimed at preventing what was still a negligible problem. It also happened to coincide with the introduction of "marihuana" from Mexico caused by the revolution and resulting immigration to Southern California. Yet even without the Mexicans, the Board would likely have proceeded to outlaw Indian hemp anyway, just like Massachusetts, Maine, Indiana, and Wyoming. Anticipatory regulation of this sort is a common feature of the modern era, as noted by sociologist Edwin Lemert in the 1950s. Lemert observed that 23 California communities "had trailer camp ordinances without, however, having any trailer camps to regulate."[168] Similarly, in recent years, numerous California cities and counties have passed ordinances to regulate (or

---

[167] Morgan, op. cit., p. 77 (like other commentators, Morgan mistakenly dates the first law to 1915).

[168] Edwin M. Lemert, "Is There a Natural History of Social Problems?" *American Sociological Review*, 16:221(1951) (thanks to Jim Baumohl for bringing this article to my attention).

prevent) non-existent cannabis dispensaries. Lemert attributed such phenomena to the power of administrative elites to anticipate and define problems and recommend solutions. Henry Finger was a charter member of this elite, starting from the very first years of the State Board of Pharmacy.

The technocratic rationale for anti-cannabis legislation had been aptly laid out for Finger by Hamilton Wright, who argued that cannabis might become popular once opium was suppressed. As it turned out, Wright's prediction was prescient: cannabis did increase in popularity, eventually far surpassing opium. Wright's prescription proved less successful. What had begun as an idle preventative project became mired in prohibitionist futility. In the years after 1913, the population of cannabis users swelled from a tiny minority to millions of Californians. In the process, the state incurred over 2,780,000 marijuana arrests, including 1,300,000 felonies.[169]

Historically, it is significant that California, a pioneer in cannabis prohibition, was likewise at the forefront of the movement to decriminalize and legalize its use. California's lengthy experience with failing to stop the marijuana trade made it all the more ripe for reform. It is also significant that the movement to re-legalize cannabis was spearheaded by popular initiatives against the almost universal opposition of public officials and law enforcement. It is a reminder that government officials have their

---

[169] Based on arrest data from the California Department of Justice Bureau of Criminal Statistics, 1960–2016.

own vested interests in upholding the laws they administer and are often removed from the values of their constituents. In the end, California's 100 Years War on cannabis was declared not on account of any public complaint, nor an evident public health problem, nor yet a Reefer Madness scare, nor anti-Mexican or other racial prejudice, nor a conspiracy against hemp, but rather a bureaucratic misadventure by a meddlesome board of pharmacy.

California Origins of Cannabis Prohibition 97

1972 California Marijuana Initiative
(Proposition 19) Sunshine Poster

State & Local Marijuana Laws, Pre-1933

State	Year	Chapter of Law	Reference
Alabama	1931	No. 26	1
Arizona	1931	Chap. 36	1
Arkansas	1923	Act 213	1
California	1913	Chap. 342	5
Colorado	1917	Chap. 39	1, 2, 11
Delaware	1933	Chap. 191	1
El Paso, Texas	1915	June 14, 1915	7
Hawaii (territory)	1914	Board of Health	12
Idaho	1927	Chap. 105	1
Illinois	1931	Chap. 38	1
Indiana	1913	March 6, 1913	3, 5
Iowa	1921	Chap. 282	1
Kansas	1927	Chap. 192	1
Louisiana	1924	July 3, 1924	3, 4
Maine	1913	Chap. 164	3, 5
Massachusetts	1911	Chap. 372	5
Michigan	1929	No. 310	1
Mississippi	1930	Chap.13	1
Missouri	1889	Rev. Stat. 3874 (hasheesh dens)	10
Montana	1927	Chap. 91	1, 2
Nebraska	1927	Chap. 145	1
Nevada	1917	Mar. 24, 1917	3, 4
New Mexico	1923	Chap. 42	1, 2
New York	1927	Chap. 692	1, 2
New York City	1914		2
North Dakota	1933	Chap. 106	1
Ohio	1927	No. 422	1
Oklahoma	1933	Chap. 24	1

Orange County, California	1917		9
Oregon	1923	Chap. 27	1
Pennsylvania	1933	No. 163	1
Portland, Oregon	1915		8
Rhode Island	1918	Chap. 1674	1
South Dakota	1931	Chap. 127	1
Texas	1919	Chap. 66	1, 2
Utah	1915	Chap. 66	1, 6
Vermont	1915	No. 197	1
Washington	1923	March 3, 1923	3, 4
Wyoming	1913	Chap. 93	3, 4

References:

A review of the standard sources on the dates of state marijuana laws reveals a few inconsistencies, errors, and omissions, which have hopefully been corrected here.

1. Bonnie and Whitebread, *The Marihuana Conviction* (Univ. of Virginia Press, Charlottesville) 1974, p. 354.
2. Bonnie and Whitebread, "The Forbidden Fruit and the Tree of Knowledge: An Inquiry into the Legal History of American Marijuana Prohibition," Part III, *Virginia Law Review* 56#6, October 1970.
3. Ron Hamowy, *Dealing With Drugs* (Lexington Books, Lexington MA) 1987, pp. 10–11.
4. Surgeon General's report, "State Laws Relating to the Control of Narcotic Drugs and the Treatment of Drug Addiction," Supplement #91 to *Public Health Reports* (1931).
5. A 1912 amended version of the law is listed in Martin Wilbert and Murray Galt Motter, , "Poisons and Habit-Forming Drugs," in *Public*

Health Reports Vol. XXVIII #41, October 10, 1913, and #42, October 17, 1913.
6. Charles Whitebread, "The History of the Non-Medical Use of Drugs in the United States," Speech to the 1995 California Judges Association annual conference, posted at www.druglibrary.org/schaffer/History/HISTORY.HTM.
7. "Marihuana Sale Now Prohibited," *El Paso Herald,* June 3, 1915, p.6.
8. "General News of the Trade," *Pacific Drug Review,* 27#7 p. 26 (July 1915).
9. "Raised Marijuana for Stomach's Sake," *Santa Ana Daily Register*, July 7, 1919, p.3; "Officers Object to 'Dream Weed' Crop," *Los Angeles Times,* July 6, 1919, V-9.
10. "Constitutionality of Law Regulating Sale of Opium*," British Medical Journal* I, June 5, 1897, p. 1092. The 1889 Missouri law outlawed opium and hasheesh dens; marijuana *per se* was not outlawed in the state until 1935: Bonnie and Whitebread, *The Marihuana Conviction,* pp. 112–4.
11. Colorado passed laws to prohibit both cultivation and sale of cannabis in 1917, but the law against sale was repealed in 1919. Sale and possession were ultimately recriminalized in 1927. Henry O. Whiteside, *Menace in the West: Colorado and the American Experience with Drugs, 1873–1963,* (Colorado Historical Society, Denver, 1997) pp. 36–9, 52–4,
12. Territorial Board of Health regulation January 15, 1914. *Honolulu Advertiser* December 15, 1913, p.7; January 24, 1914, p.11.

About the Author

Dale Gieringer has been the state director of the California chapter of the National Organization for the Reform of Marijuana Laws (California NORML) since 1987. In this capacity, he has advocated, written, and lobbied for the responsible legal availability of cannabis. He is also a member of the national NORML board of directors. He wrote his PhD dissertation on "Consumer Choice and FDA Drug Regulation" at Stanford and has published original research on the medical uses of cannabis, the history of cannabis and drug prohibition, the economic costs and benefits of legalization, THC potency and CBD testing, marijuana and driving safety, and the use of vaporization as a smoke-free delivery system for cannabis. He is the author of *Marijuana Medical Handbook* (2008) and *California NORML Guide to Drug Testing* (2013). He was one of the original co-authors of California's 1996 medical marijuana initiative, Proposition 215, and the proponent of Oakland's Measure Z adult use cannabis initiative in 2004. He was a founding member of ProjectCBD, which pioneered the re-introduction of CBD into cannabis medicine. He is a member of the International Association for Cannabinoid Medicine, the Society of Cannabis Clinicians, and the advisory board of the California Center for Medicinal Cannabis Research. He is a board member of the California Cannabis Historical Society, devoted to preserving the history of the cannabis movement in California.

CAcannabishistoricalsociety.org

Index

Adult Use of Marijuana Act, 89
Alabama, 98
Alameda County, 24
Alcohol, 17, 28, 42, 44, 57, 70, 71, 78, 86, 91
Anslinger, Harry, 43, 81, 85, 92
Arabs, 23, 24, 25
Arizona, 35, 36, 41, 56, 98
Arkansas, 98
Armenians, 23, 25, 26, 76
Asian, 34, 55
Board of Pharmacy, 6, 7, 28, 45, 50, 57, 60, 68, 76, 91, 94, 95
Bonnie and Whitebread, 41, 99, 100
Boston, 19, 21, 26, 55, 76
Bowers, W.W., 22
Brent, Bishop, 52
British, 22, 36, 40, 44, 55, 56, 100
British Indian Hemp Drugs Commission, 55
Butte County, 10, 30
California Board of Pharmacy, 6, 54, 61, 76
California College of Pharmacy, 30, 50, 64
California Marijuana Initiative, 87, 97
California Pharmaceutical Association, 63
California State Board of Trade, 24
Campaign Against Marijuana Planting, 88
Campos, Isaac, 4, 35, 36, 42, 93
Cannabis indica, 8, 10, 18, 19, 30, 33, 39, 43, 44, 65, 68, 70, 76
Cannabis sativa, 8, 10, 33, 68

Catholic, 9
Central Valley, 10, 25, 53, 55
Chicago, 21, 50, 81
Chinatown, 20, 45, 52
Chinese, 6, 20, 44, 55, 93
Club des Haschischins, 11
Colorado, 89, 98, 100
Congress, 7, 43, 57, 58, 65
Daggett, Rollin Mallory, 18
Delaware, 98
Department of Agriculture, 33, 67, 68, 77
Deveny, Peter, 22
Egypt, 11, 29, 40
El Paso, 9, 77, 78, 98, 100
Emerald Triangle, 88
Federal Bureau of Narcotics, 80, 81
Finger, Henry J., 50, 51, 52, 53, 54, 56, 58, 59, 60, 63, 64, 69, 70, 80, 93, 94, 95
French, 11, 17, 39
Fresno, 9, 56, 59
Gillett, James, 44, 51

Gold Rush, 11, 20
Golden Age, 18
Grass Valley, 17
Harrison Act, 7, 46, 47, 51, 69
Harte, Bret, 15
Hasheesh Infant, 16
Hawaii, 18, 98
Hearst, William Randolph, 43, 51, 78, 79, 92, 93
Hemp, 8, 9, 10, 11, 19, 21, 22, 24, 25, 26, 30, 41, 43, 46, 52, 54, 55, 56, 57, 58, 59, 60, 61, 63, 64, 65, 66, 67, 68, 71, 72, 73, 75, 80, 81, 91, 92, 93, 94, 96
Hindoo, 27, 32, 56
Hindoos, 53, 55, 57, 70, 93
Indian hemp, 8, 22, 58, 68
Indiana, 76, 94, 98
International Conference on Opium, 51
Kentucky, 33
La Cucaracha, 42
Lebanese, 25, 26, 27
Lemert, Edwin, 94
Livermore, 24, 25

Loco weed, 35, 60, 61, 68, 84
London, 19, 28, 39, 52
Long Beach, 78
Los Angeles, 9, 10, 27, 35, 36, 40, 41, 42, 59, 60, 69, 72, 73, 74, 78, 79, 82, 84, 86, 91, 100
Love, James, 38, 87
Ludlow, Fitz Hugh, 12, 13, 15, 16, 17, 18, 19
Madagascar, 33
Maine, 76, 94, 98
Mariguana, 8, 35, 36, 41
Marihuana, 8, 34, 35, 36, 38, 39, 40, 41, 42, 43, 56, 59, 62, 73, 74, 75, 76, 78, 82, 84, 85, 86, 91, 93, 94
Marihuana Tax Act, 6, 43, 47, 81, 85, 91
Marihuano, 60, 62
Massachusetts, 76, 80, 94, 98
Mexican, 8, 35, 36, 37, 40, 41, 42, 59, 60, 61, 62, 67, 68, 72, 73, 74, 75, 77, 78, 79, 81, 82, 86, 91, 92, 96
Mexico, 34, 35, 36, 37, 38, 39, 40, 41, 59, 60, 61, 62, 76, 93, 94, 98
Middle East, 26, 39
Mississippi, 33, 98
Morphine, 7, 17, 22, 45, 58, 62, 63, 67, 68, 75, 78, 82
Moscone Act, 87
Nahon, S.A., 23, 24, 25
Nevada County, 17, 22
New Orleans, 9, 21, 59
New York, 2, 9, 10, 11, 15, 19, 20, 21, 26, 35, 36, 39, 43, 46, 56, 61, 76, 77, 92, 98
Nogales, 41
Opium, 7, 16, 17, 20, 21, 22, 23, 35, 38, 44, 45, 46, 52, 57, 61, 62, 64, 67, 68, 74, 75, 80, 93, 95, 100
Orange County, 74, 99
Oregon, 30, 77, 99
O'Shaughnessy, William, 10, 34
Ottoman Empire, 26
Pacific Drug Review, 29, 33, 36, 38, 50, 63, 64, 67, 77, 90, 100

Pacific Pharmacist and *Pacific Drug Review*, 29
Panama, 36, 43, 56
Peron, Dennis, 88
Philadelphia, 11, 18, 21, 33, 36, 41, 80
Poison Law, 6, 63, 64, 68
Progressive Era, 6, 34, 44, 94
Proposition 215, 88, 102
Proposition 64, 89
Proposition P, 88
Pure Food and Drugs Act, 44
Reefer Madness, 21, 41, 42, 43, 79, 85, 92, 93, 96
Republican, 50
Retail Druggists' Association, 64
Robinson, Victor, 34
Roosevelt, Theodore, 45
Sacramento, 9, 10, 19, 21, 22, 23, 29, 69, 75, 76, 82, 84, 85
San Diego, 9, 22, 36, 61
San Francisco, 6, 8, 9, 10, 14, 15, 16, 17, 19, 20, 21, 22, 23, 27, 29, 30, 34, 35, 45, 46, 50, 51, 55, 56, 64, 66, 68, 69, 71, 75, 76, 79, 81, 82, 84, 87, 88
Santa Cruz, 56
Schneider, Albert, 30, 31, 70
Shanghai, 44, 52
Sikhs, 55
Spanish, 9, 10, 76
State Narcotic Committee Report, 83
Sterling, George, 28, 29
Stockton, 9, 23, 24, 25, 27, 40
Syria, 11
Syrians, 25, 26, 67, 93
Taylor, Bayard, 11, 34
Texas, 38, 68, 77, 98, 99
The Hasheesh Eater, 12, 15, 16, 19
Tobacco, 17, 19, 26, 35, 36, 37, 40, 75, 86
Turks, 23, 25, 26, 76
Twain, Mark, 14, 15, 16, 18

US Department of Agriculture Bureau of Plant Industry, 33
US Pharmacopoeia, 33
Utah, 76, 99
Vermont, 76, 99
Villa, Pancho, 41, 42
Virginia City, 18

Washington, 10, 26, 35, 36, 39, 42, 61, 80, 89, 99
West Indies, 56
World War I, 6, 25, 33, 34, 76, 92
Wright, Hamilton, 26, 45, 46, 48, 52, 58, 59, 60, 63, 65, 95
Wyoming, 76, 94, 99

www.ingramcontent.com/pod-product-compliance
Lightning Source LLC
LaVergne TN
LVHW021403080426
835508LV00020B/2428